ABOUT THE AUTHOR

STEPHAN M. HORAK, born in Western Ukraine, attended Polish public schools until 1939 and completed his secondary education under Russian occupation where he had his first experience with the Soviet system of government. After World War II he studied at the Universities of Erlangen and Bonn, Germany, and upon receiving the Ph.D. degree in 1949, taught history for several years. In 1953 he joined the East European Institute at the University of Tübingen, Germany, as a research fellow under the late Professor Werner Markert. In 1956 he came to the United States and received the degree of M.A. in Library Science from the University of Michigan in 1960. In the same year he was appointed Slavic librarian at Indiana University. He returned to teaching in 1964, first at the University of Kentucky and Vanderbilt University, joining the faculty of Eastern Illinois University in 1965 where he teaches European and Russian history.

Dr. Horak's published works include: *Poland's International Affairs, 1919-1960; A Calendar; Poland and Her National Minorities, 1919-1939; Ukraine in der internationalen Politik; Russia's Historical Way to Bolshevism; Die Ukraine 1917-1920 und Deutschland: Bündnis und Enttäuschung.* He contributed numerous articles to professional journals and presented several papers to professional meetings including the American Historical Association and American Association for the Advancement of Slavic Studies.

East European Area Studies Series, No. 1

JUNIOR SLAVICA

JUNIOR SLAVICA

A Selected Annotated Bibliography
of Books in English
on Russia and Eastern Europe

Compiled by
STEPHAN M. HORAK
Eastern Illinois University

1968
LIBRARIES UNLIMITED, INC.
Rochester, N. Y.

Libraries Unlimited, Inc.
P. O. Box 9842
Rochester, New York 14623

Printed in the United States of America

To my wife and children

CONTENTS

PART II

EASTERN EUROPE — GENERAL

PART III

BALKAN PENINSULA — GENERAL

PART IV

EASTERN EUROPE BY COUNTRIES

INTRODUCTION

This bibliography is necessary for many reasons, not the least of which is the growing popularity of Russian and East European studies in colleges and secondary schools. The flood of publications in recent years has reached a stage of confusion for those in the field of teaching and library acquisitions. According to my estimate, there were published in this country in the last decade over two thousand titles dealing either directly or indirectly with Russia and East Europe. Few libraries can afford to acquire all this material. The great majority, for one or another reason, must operate selectively and within self-imposed limitations.

Hence, this selected bibliography of over 600 titles is intended primarily to fulfill the needs of liberal arts and teacher colleges. Junior colleges and high schools will find many titles in this guide which are important for their respective curricula. By the same token, public libraries which must respond to increasing requests for material on Russian and East European affairs will find a useful selection of books.

Existing bibliographies which are similar in content, including Sergius Yakobson's Five Hundred Works for College Libraries, Washington, 1948, are outdated or were compiled for another reason. Some of the more recent bibliographies are tools for the researcher and thus highly specialized. In contrast, this bibliography was designed to emphasize material useful in teaching and learning on the undergraduate level. Junior Slavica will be a helpful guide in college libraries which must maintain an adequate number of titles to support instructional offerings in this particular field of studies. In junior colleges this bibliography may serve as the nucleus of a desirable Slavic collection, while in some large high schools, it should become the foundation for purchasing the most valuable and purposeful titles. These considerations essentially determined the process of selection of titles which are included in Junior Slavica.

The selection itself, in view of the above limitations, does not claim to be complete. Many important publications due to their specialization are judged unsuitable for an undergraduate program. Others, and these are in the majority, do not contribute significantly to the process of education. Selection is restricted to works in the English language. In this country we have already reached a point where it is possible to support Russian and East European studies with a literature solely in English. Some unavoidable shortcomings in some areas can be overcome by use of general textbooks. Hopefully, existing gaps will soon be filled by a growing number of scholarly contributions. If Junior Slavica suggests the still neglected areas, it will justify its value as a guide.

Among existing bibliographies, Junior Slavica claims a position between Robert F. Byrnes' Bibliography of American Publications on East Central Europe, 1945-1957 (1958) and Paul Horecky's Russia and the Soviet Union: A Bibliographic Guide to Western-Language Publications (1965). Junior Slavica, to a certain degree, continues the work of the first title, whereas the latter's very purpose differs considerably. Hence, it does not duplicate either; but rather intends to fill a gap between the two.

The arrangement, selection and coverage of Junior Slavica warrants a short explanation to render this tool more useful. The compiler's experience as a teacher and Slavic librarian enabled him to select the necessary books most useful for teachers and students. In addition, many distinguished specialists in their respective fields generously responded to a questionaire, thereby assuring a more balanced coverage of areas outside the author's field of specialization. The author extends sincere thanks and appreciation to all whose names are listed at the end of this introduction.

A third source, reviews from leading professional journals, frequently served as a decisive factor in choosing a title. The overwhelming number of entries are accompanied by annotations based on excerpts from reviews. To acknowledge the indirect contribution of reviewers, their names are given under each annotation. Occasionally, these quotations were abridged or complemented at the compiler's discretion.

The purpose of identifying the location of the review is to help the user of this bibliography arrive at his own decision: for the librarian in ordering a specific title for the library collection; for the instructor in suggesting a particular book to a student; and for the student in selecting a particular title for study. In each case the user may consult the original review and obtain the opinion of an expert with a minimum of searching. With this in mind, Junior Slavica is comparable to the purpose and methodology used by the Book Review Digest, Bibliographic Index.

As indicated previously, Junior Slavica is also intended for high school libraries. The importance of this objective can be illustrated by recognizing the fact that the Standard Catalog for High School Libraries (8th ed., 1962), lists only four titles under the heading "USSR and Russia" and only one book can be found under "Hungary". This otherwise handy bibliography has thus left a wide gap in these vital areas. It appears superfluous to dwell on this lamentable situation in 1968. Suffice it to say, that similar catalogs for college libraries have not fared much better.

As one will notice, the majority of titles listed in this bibliography were published during the last decade. This fact, first of all, attests to the mushrooming interest of almost all disciplines in the Slavic area. To explain this phenomenon it is recommended that one read "An Appraisal of Russian Studies in the United States," The American Slavic and East European Review, Vol. 18, No. 2, pp. 417-441 . This report was written by a panel of our leading experts on Soviet Russia and Eastern Europe, including Cyril E. Black, Robert F. Byrnes, Charles Jelavich, Donald W. Treadgold and John M. Thompson, in the capacity of the "Subcommittee on the Review of Russian Studies." They produced an exhaustive report of American achievements for the years 1945-1956. From the perspective of 1968 the effort appears less impressive. Nevertheless, it served its purpose well by calling our attention to the importance of greater concentration on this vital issue.

Junior Slavica, to a certain extent, illustrates the achievements of the second period (1956-1968) as a living monument to American scholarship. Within this second phase the United States rose to the position of unchallenged leader in the field of Russian and East European area studies outside the geographical boundaries of that part of the world.

Indeed, an impressive academic achievement has been displayed in the last fifty years by American scholars in the East European field. It is well to remember that the first history of Russia was published in 1905 in this country by R. van Bergen, The Story of Russia, New York, American Book Co., 288p. In the preface Mr. van Bergen observed: "Recent events have drawn the attention upon Russia, a country of which but little is known here, because the intercourse between it and the United States has been limited."

Sixty-two years later as this bibliography, in part, bears witness, many changes occurred not only in Russia, but in this country as well. We can certainly support our claim of knowing more about Russia than our grandfathers did.

A limited number of scholarly works dating from that first period are included in this bibliography. However, many books published prior to 1956 are outdated or are replaced by more valuable contributions during the last decade.

This compiler also took into consideration the current availability of a listed title; a bibliography of books which are out-of-print presents certain problems to libraries building up a particular collection, or even for a bookstore trying to satisfy the demand. Thus, Junior Slavica was checked against Books in Print to assure the user that a chosen work is still available.

This bibliography admits a priori its arbitrary limitation to the disciplines of the social sciences, comprising history, philosophy, sociology, education, government, political science, geography and economics, as well as the broad area of general reference, including some important bibliographies. Articles are excluded in order to adhere to the purpose as outlined in the subtitle of Junior Slavica. Articles in English are well indexed in The American Bibliography of Russian and East European Studies, published by Indiana University in its "Russian and East European Series."

Another technical limitation arose from geographical considerations. To many the term "Eastern Europe" is too vague, therefore, some observations are justified. The geographical area of "Eastern Europe", as it is used in the context of this bibliography, includes the following states as they are existing since World War II: Poland, Czechoslovakia, Hungary, Rumania, Yugoslavia, Albania, Bulgaria, and the USSR, with all non-Russian Soviet republics (Estonia, Latvia, Lithuania, Belorussia, Ukraine, Moldavia, Azerbajdzan, Armenia, Georgia, and to a lesser degree, the republics of Central Asia). Historical considerations are responsible for such subject headings as Mongols, Ottoman Empire and Austria-Hungary, while Byzantium and Greece are omitted simply because they do not constitute a part of the Russian and East European Area Studies offered at our major universities. Consequently, contemporary Austria and even the Soviet Zone of Germany, the German Democratic Republic, are not included either, though the latter is frequently within the range of discussion of communism and the Soviet sphere of influence.

Abbreviations used in the Junior Slavica are as follows:

AHR - The American Historical Review

CSP - Canadian Slavonic Papers

CSS - Canadian Slavic Studies

EE - East Europe

EEQ - East European Quarterly

JMH - The Journal of Modern History

R - Reviewer

SEEJ - The Slavic and East European Journal

SEER - The Slavonic and East European Review (London)

SR - American Slavic and East European Review, now known as Slavic Review

In conclusion, I wish to express my sincere gratitude to those experts who suggested titles which they regard as significant contributions in their disciplines: Jeremy Anderson, John Armstrong, Frederick C. Barghoorn, Samuel B. Baron, Peter A. Berton, Cyril E. Black, Joseph Brožek, Robert V. Daniels, Nicholas De Witt, Walter M. Drzewieniecki, M. Kamil Dziewanowski, Sidney Harcave, Chancy D. Harris, Charles Morley, Nicholas V. Riasanovsky, Ivo J. Lederer and Joseph F. Zacek.

The beforementioned journals, too, deserve my acknowledgement for granting me permission to quote from their reviews and last, but not least, my gratitude to the Research Committee of Eastern Illinois University which gave me the financial support for this project.

The compiler invites suggestions and comments on this bibliography, in the hope that a second edition will be free of any shortcomings which may have escaped detection of this edition of <u>Junior Slavica</u>.

S. M. H.

January, 1968.

CHAPTER I

RUSSIA AND USSR

RUSSIA UNTIL 1917

A. Bibliographies

(See also Bibliographies, USSR)

1. HORECKY, Paul L. ed. Russia and the Soviet Union: A Bibliographic Guide to Western-Language Publications. Chicago, University of Chicago Press, 1965. 473p. $8.95.

   > A collection of 1960 entries of publications in western languages.

   > SEER, Vol. 9, No. 4, pp. 470-74
   > R: Waclaw W. Soroka

2. MAICHEL, Karol. Guide to Russian Reference Books. Volume I: General Bibliographies and Reference Books. Edited by J. S. G. Simmons. Stanford, The Hoover Institution on War, Revolution and Peace, Stanford University, 1962. 92p. $5.00 (Hoover Institution Bibliographical Series, No. 10)

   > SR, Vol. 23, No. 1, pp. 179-81.
   > R: R. A. Karlowich

3. MAICHEL, Karol. Guide to Russian Reference Books. Volume II: History, Auxiliary Historical Sciences, Ethnography, and Geography. Edited by J. S. G. Simmons. Stanford, The Hoover Institution on War, Revolution and Peace, Stanford

University, 1964. 297p. $12.00. (Hoover Institution Bibliographical Series, No. 18)

> SR, Vol. 25, No. 2, pp. 370-372.
> R: Fritz T. Epstein

B. Biographies

3a. BARON, Samuel H. ed. and transl. The Travels of Olearius in Seventeenth-Century Russia. Stanford, Stanford University Press, 1967. 400p. $10.00.

> This is a firsthand account of the travels of Adam Oelschlager, better known as Olearius, through Muscovy and Tartary from 1633 to 1636. Olearius, a young German, served as secretary to successive embassies sent by the Duke of Holstein to the Tsar of Russia and the Shah of Persia to negotiate trade agreements. The book includes sixteen pages of the original illustrations, which were based on Olearius's own drawings. This account is essential to the study of Russia's history.

4. HARE, Richard. Portraits of Russian Personalities Between Reform and Revolution. New York, London, Oxford University Press, 1959. 360p. $6.75.

> The book contains fifteen sketches of varying lengths treating Turgenev, Dostoevsky, Tolstoy and lesser known figures such as the narodniks N. Mikhailovsky, P. Lavrov, L. Tikhomirov. The essays are readable, informative and often stimulating because of a point of view that challenges more commonly accepted historical portraits.

> AHR, Vol. 65, No. 1, pp. 180-81.
> R: George Barr Carson, Jr.

C. Description and Travel

5. FLETCHER, Giles. Of the Rus' Commonwealth.
    Edited by Albert J. Schmidt. Ithaca, N. Y.,
    Cornell University Press, 1966. 224p. $6.00.
    (Folger Documents of Tudor and Stuart Civiliza-
    tion)

    Originally published in 1591, this is a vivid
    discourse on the national resources, the
    government, ecclesiastical and military
    organization and the class structure of
    Russian society as observed by a British
    traveler.

6. KOHLER, Phyllis Penn. ed. and transl. Journey
    for Our Time: Selections from the Journals of the
    Marquis de Custine. New York, Pellegrini &
    Cudahy, 1951. 338p. $4.00.

    An account of Russian autocracy of Nicholas
    I by a French aristocrat who came to the
    country as an admirer and left it as an
    enemy. It contains much valuable informa-
    tion but is marked by some errors.

7. STADEN, Heinrich von. The Land and Government
    of Muscovy: A Sixteenth-Century Account. Trans-
    lated and edited by Thomas Esper. Stanford, Calif.,
    Stanford University Press, 1967. 142p. $5.50.

    A report by a German adventurer who went
    to Russia in the 1560's and spent three years
    in the service of Ivan the Terrible's
    Oprichnina. The author had an eye for in-
    teresting details. His unique account has
    thus always attracted the attention of west-
    ern historians. An asset to any college
    library.

D. Historiography

8.   MAZOUR, Anatole G. Modern Russian Historiography. 2nd ed. Princeton, N. J., Van Nostrand, 1958. 260p. $6.50.

>A thoroughly competent study which covers nearly all Russian historians of significance before and after the October Revolution. This volume fills an urgent need and is unique in American scholarly literature. A must for any library.
>
>SR, Vol. 18, No. 2, pp. 250-52.
>R: Marc Szeftel

E. History — Atlases

9.   ADAMS, Arthur et al. An Atlas of Russian and East European History. New York, Praeger, 1967. 204p. $6.00, cloth. $2.25, paper.

>Through more than 100 maps and a completely integrated text, the authors trace both the growth of Russia and the kaleidoscopic history of Eastern Europe. Subjects discussed: geography, national groups, religious diversity, economy, politics and cultural development. Indispensable reference book for students and teachers. Important for high school and college libraries.

10.   CHEW, Allen F. An Atlas of Russian History: Eleven Centuries of Changing Borders. New Haven, London, Yale University Press, 1967. 113p. $3.95, paper; spiral binding.

>This atlas is an essential supplement to the study of Russian history. It contains thirty-four maps, each accompanied by concise, descriptive text.

F.   History — Sources and Documents

11.   HOWES, Robert Craig. ed. and transl.   The Testa-
ments of the Grand Princes of Moscow.   Ithaca,
N. Y. , Cornell University Press, 1967.   486p.
$10. 00.

>   A most vital information about medieval
>   Russia is here made available in English
>   for the first time.   The testaments of the
>   Grand Princes of Moscow, from Ivan I to
>   Ivan IV, disclose the territorial gains and
>   ensuing power which made Ivan the Terrible
>   "autocrat of all Rus'. "

12.   PIPES, Richard. ed. Karamzin's Memoir an Ancient
and Modern Russia: A Translation and Analysis.
Cambridge, Harvard University Press, 1959.   2
Vols.   Volume I: Introduction and translated text.
166p.   Volume II: Russian text.   119p. $5. 50 both
vols.   (Harvard Russian Research Center Studies,
Nos. 33, 34)

>   The Memoir was written for the Grand
>   Duchess Catherine and given by her to her
>   brother, Alexander I.   It was rediscovered
>   in the papers of Arakcheiev in 1835.   The
>   whole text was not available to the Russian
>   public until after 1905.   This is an important
>   source in Russian history.
>
>   SEER, Vol. 39, No. 92, pp. 258-59.
>   R: H. Seton-Watson

13.   The Russian Primary Chronicle: Laurentian Text
(Povest' vremennykh let).   Translated and edited by
Samuel H. Cross and Olgerd P. Sherbowitz-Wetzor.
Cambridge, Mass. , Medieval Academy of America,
1953.   313p. $5. 00 (Medieval Academy of America,
No. 60)

>   Translation of a source of major importance,

14.   Slovo o polku Igoreve. The Song of Igor's Campaign:
      An Epic of the Twelfth Century. Translated from
      Old Russian by Vladimir Nabokov. New York,
      Vintage Books, 1960. 134p. $ 0. 95.

              An essential literary and historical document
              of the twelfth century. Suggested reading for
              students interested in the medieval history of
              the Eastern Slavs.

              G. History — General

      (Books and readers listed here cover, in most
      cases, all periods of Russian history, including to
      various degrees, the Soviet period.)

15.   BARBOUR, Philip L. Dimitry, Called the Preten-
      der: Tsar and Grand Prince of All Russia, 1605-
      1606. Boston, Houghton Mifflin, 1966. 387p.
      $6. 95.

              This well-written study contains the story of
              the first pretender of the Russian throne.
              The nonspecialist and the beginning student
              will find this version most fascinating and
              profitable for a better understanding of
              events commonly described as a "time of
              trouble. "

16.   CHARQUES, Richard D. A Short History of Russia.
      New York, Dutton, 1956. 284p. $3. 95.

              This is one of the best textbooks on Russian
              history for high school students, in particu-
              lar for the beginner.

              SR, Vol. 27, No. 3, pp. 352-53.
              R: Stanley J. Zyzniewski

17.   CLARKSON, Jesse D. A History of Russia. New
      York, Random House, 1961. 875p. $10. 00.

Balanced yet comprehensive treatment of
Russian history is evenly divided into three
parts: the first covering Russia from its
earliest time to the reign of Peter I, the
second comprising the two centuries of
Imperial Russia up to the Revolution. The
book is well written and provides understanding of the forces that molded Russian
history. It contains chapters on literature,
art, and science. Non-Russian peoples of
that empire, other than Jews, are rather
neglected. Many photos and maps enhance
this work.

SR, Vol. 21, No. 2, pp. 343-44.
R: A. Lobavov-Rostovsky

18. ELLISON, Herbert J. A History of Russia. New
York, London. Holt, Rinehart and Winston, 1964.
656p. $9.95.

From a growing list of textbooks on Russian
history, this one deserves high priority as
text for undergraduate study. Even advanced high school students will easily understand it. Contrary to similar publications,
this one devotes appropriate attention to
the national minorities in the Russian empire and the Soviet Union. A few notice-
able errors do not mar the importance of
this title.

SR, 24, No. 2, pp. 323-24.
R: Sergei Pushkarev

19. FLORINSKY, Michael T. Russia: A History and An
Interpretation. New York, Macmillan, 1954. 2 Vols.
$15.00.

One of the outstanding works on Russian
history in any western language. Critical
and equally analytical, the book deals with
the history from its beginning to 1918.
Recommended for advanced courses in

Russian history. Social, cultural, economic
and nationality aspects are not sacrificed for
political history.

SR, Vol. 13, No. 3, pp. 432-35.
R: Anatole G. Mazour

20.   FLORINSKY, Michael T. Russia: A Short History.
New York, Macmillan, 1964. 653p. $8.50.

This one-volume survey of Russian history
from its beginnings to 1963 fits well into an
undergraduate program. It is readable and
at the same time critical enough to offer the
student an objective picture of Russia. The
book maintains a periodizational balance and
can be adapted to two semesters. Especially
suitable for survey courses. Advanced high
school students should also benefit from it.

21.   HARCAVE, Sidney. ed. Readings in Russian History. Volume I: From Ancient Times to the Aboli-
tion of Serfdom. Volume II: The modern Period.
New York, Crowell, 1962. 388 and 330p. $3.75
per vol.

This very useful collection contains fifty
selections dealing with various subjects in
Russian history. Each item is related to
its historical background by a brief introduction. Many translations are for the
first time available in English.

SEEJ, Vol. 8, No. 1, p. 108.
R: Oswald P. Backus

22.   HARCAVE, Sidney. Russia: A History. Chicago,
Lippincott, 1952. 668p. $6.00.

Among the first American textbooks of
Russian history adaptable to teaching in
U.S. colleges. The author places particular stress on the most recent period and
has provided a text which is easy to follow.

Harcave takes a primarily political approach
to history, although other areas are men-
tioned. Sixteen maps and thirty-one illustrations, together with five chronological
overviews, a useful bibliography and a full
index, add favorable to the value of this
text as an undergraduate reference work.

SR, Vol. 14, No. 1, pp. 126-28.
R: Cyril E. Black

23.   HOETZSCH, Otto. The Evolution of Russia. Translated from German by Rhys Evans. New York,
Harcourt, Brace & World, 1966. 214p. $5.50,
cloth; $3.25, paper.

Well balanced survey of Russia's development. The determining influence of geographical and racial factors, and of Russia's changing relationship with Western
Europe, are the basic themes of the book.
Highly recommended for high school
libraries, teachers and as a textbook.

24.   KELLER, Werner. East Minus West ⁼ Zero:
Russia's Debt to the Western World, 1862-1962.
Translated by Constantin Fitzgibbon. New York,
Putnam's, 1962. 384p. $6.95.

The purpose of this book by a popular German writer is to prove that the major
achievements of the Russians, especially
in the arts and sciences, are due entirely
to the knowledge they have borrowed,
stolen, or otherwise appropriated from
the West over the course of centuries, or
have been produced by foreigners in the
service of Russia.

SR, Vol. 22, No. 1, pp. 148-49.
R: Stuart R. Tompkins

25.   RIASANOVSKY, Nicholas V. A History of Russia.
New York, London, Oxford University Press,

1963. 711p. $8.00.

Riasanovsky's textbook is well organized along simple chronological lines and for the most part provides essential and reliable information on salient aspects of Russia's historical evolution. The account is lucid and tends to favor the more conservative interpretations. Primarily designed for college students but useful for advanced high school students.

SR, Vol. 22, No. 4, pp. 753-54.
R: Michael T. Florinsky

26. RICE, Tamara T. A Concise History of Russian Art. New York, Praeger, 1963. 288p. $7.50, cloth; $3.95, paper.

This book is a survey of the visual arts of Russia, or more directly, of the Eastern Slavs, from pre-Christian times to the beginning of the Soviet period. Subjects treated include the minor arts, hagiography, architecture and painting. A useful addition for supplemental reading in Russian history, language and subject studies.

SEEJ, Vol. 8, No. 4, pp. 472-73.
R: Ira Eppler

27. RIHA, Thomas. Readings in Russian Civilization. Vol. I: 900-1700; Vol. II: 1700-1917; Vol. III: 1917-1963. Chicago, University of Chicago Press, 1964. 3 Vols. in 1. $12.50 or $3.75 each.

This selection includes religious, literary, philosophic, economic, ideological and political aspects of Russian history. As of now, an unsurpassed reader which can be successfully applied to lower and upper levels of Russian area studies.

28. SENN, Alfred E. Readings in Russian Political and Diplomatic History. Vol. I: The Tsarist

Period; Vol. II: The Soviet Period. Homewood,
Ill., The Dorsey Press, 1966. 2 Vols. $3.50 per
volume, paper.

> Well-balanced selection of material arranged
> in chronological order. Recommended for
> reading in survey courses of Russian history.

29.   SPECTOR, Ivar and Marion Spector. eds. Readings
in Russian History and Culture. Boston, Allyn and
Bacon, 1965. 489p. $2.95, paper.

> This volume comprises sixty-three readings,
> stressing historical and cultural aspects of
> Russian life. A substantial number of the
> selections has been translated into English
> for the first time by the editors. They
> have also provided appropriate up-to-date
> introductions to each selection. Suitable
> for undergraduates. High School students
> can also use this handy reader.

30.   STURLY, D. M. A Short History of Russia. London, Longmans, Green & Co., 1964. 310p. 25s.

> Written for British secondary schools, this
> book can be successfully utilized in Ameri-
> can high schools, but is most appropriate
> in junior colleges for survey courses.

31.   VERNADSKY, George and Michael Karpovich. A
History of Russia. Fifth rev. ed. New Haven,
Yale University Press, 1961. 512p. $8.50, cloth;
$2.95, paper.

> One of the most comprehensive histories of
> Russia available in English. The authors
> underline the Mongol influences upon Rus-
> sia and her national character.

32.   WALSH, Warren B. comp. and ed. Readings in
Russian History: From Ancient Times to the
Post-Stalin Era. 4th ed., extensively rev. Vol. I:
From Ancient Times to the Eighteenth Century. 244p.

Vol. II: From the Reign of Paul to Alexander III. 245p.; Vol. III: The Revolutionary Era and the Soviet Period. 535p. Syracuse, N. Y., Syracuse University Press, 1963. $6.95, paper.

> SR, Vol. 23, No. 3, pp. 578-79.
> R: Ralph T. Fisher, Jr.

H. History — Muscovy and Moscow Period

33. DMYTRYSHYN, Basil. ed. Medieval Russia: A Source Book, 900-1700. New York, Holt, Rinehart & Winston, 1967. 320p. $4.95, paper.

> Forty-one excerpts from various sources make this volume indispensable to the English-speaking student as it provides translated original material which would not be accessible otherwise. Maps and a well-selected bibliography are included.

34. FENNELL, John L. I. ed. and transl. The Correspondence Between Prince A. M. Kurbsky and Tsar Ivan IV of Russia, 1564-1579. New York, Cambridge University Press, 1955. 275p. $6.50.

> This edited correspondence between Prince Kurbsky and Ivan the Terrible presents an annotated text of the original letters and also provides the first English translation. The main value of the correspondence is its evidence of the controversy between absolutism and the older aristocracy in sixteenth-century Muscovy. Essential title for the student of Russian history.
>
> JMH, Vol. 28, No. 2, p. 211.
> R: G. B. C.

35. FENNELL, John L. I. Ivan the Great of Moscow. New York, St. Martin's Press, 1961. 386p. $12.00

This study is primarily concerned with the diplomacy and military ventures as well as the remarkable territorial expansion of Muscovy-Russia between 1462 and 1505. Because of the significance of that period in Russia's past, this detailed study deserves a place in a basic bibliography of Russia's history. The author has presented fresh views on the rule of Ivan III.

SR, Vol. 22, No. 1, pp. 139-40.
R: Gustave Alef

36. FENNELL, John L. I. ed. and transl. <u>Prince</u> A. M. Kurbsky's History of Ivan IV. New York, Cambridge University Press, 1965. 313p. $12.50.

This first English translation of Kurbsky's History is ably and commendably rendered. Explanatory notes complement this some-times misleading and often difficult source. The paucity of reliable documentation for much of the period of Ivan IV's reign makes Kurbsky's History an indispensable work.

AHR, Vol. 71, No. 2, pp. 625-26.
R: Gustave Alef

36a. GREY, Ian. <u>Ivan III and the Unification of Russia.</u> New York, Macmillan, 1967. 181p. $1.25, paper.

The book illuminates the crucial years of the fifteenth century which saw the further ex-pansion of Muscovy under Ivan III.

37. VOYCE, Arthur. <u>Moscow and the Roots of Russian Culture.</u> Norman, University of Oklahoma Press, 1964. 194p. $2.75.

A useful and carefully balanced analysis of the daily life of the Muscovites and the broader web of their family and public re-lations is sketched. It draws a clear pic-ture of the all-pervasive religious sentiment.

A solid contribution to better understanding
of the history of Russian culture. Students
in high school and junior college will enjoy
reading this particular presentation.

SEEJ, Vol. 10, No. 3, pp. 369-70.
R: Alexander Vucinich

I. History — Mongols

38.   PRAVDIN, Michael. The Mongol Empire: Its
       Rise and Legacy. Translated from the German
       by Eden and Cedar Paul. 2nd ed. New York, The
       Free Press, 1967. 581p. $2.95, paper.

              Still the most accurate and authoritative
              account on the rise and fall of the world's
              largest empire. It describes the ascent of
              the Mongol people, who, through the mili-
              tary genius of one man, overwhelmed and
              subdued the nations of half of the world.
              The book underlines the influence of Asia
              upon Europe in general, and on Russia in
              particular.

39.   VERNADSKY, George. The Mongols and Russia.
       New Haven, Yale University Press, 1953. 462p.
       $7.50.

              This study traces the Mongol empire which
              has changed the path of history of the East-
              ern Slavs and perhaps of Europe. Moscow
              grew more powerful as the Russians came
              to realize that only a strong ruler could
              repel the Mongols, and the princes of
              Moscow proved to be stronger than their
              rivals.

              SR, Vol. 13, No. 4, pp. 606-8.
              R: Harold H. Fisher

J. History — Imperial Russia until 1917

40. ADAMS, Arthur E. ed. Imperial Russia After 1861: Peaceful Modernization or Revolution? Boston, Heath, 1965. 108p. $1.50. (Problems in European Civilization)

> Selection of articles dealing with various aspects of Russian social, intellectual and political life after 1861. A competent introduction guides the reader by outlining basic issues and points of views with which the essays deal. A well-documented bibliography is appended.
>
> CSS, Vol. 1, pp. 137-38.
> R: Rex A. Wade

41. BROWDER, Robert P. and Alexander F. Kerensky. eds. The Russian Provisional Government, 1917. Documents. Stanford, Stanford University Press, 1961. 3 Vols. $30.00. (Hoover Institution Publications)

> Collection of documents of Russia and other countries, in particular of British and American origin, pertaining to the short-lived Provisional Government of Russian affairs are given a new source material not readily accessible otherwise.

42. CHARQUES, Richard D. The Twilight of Imperial Russia. Fair Lawn, N.J., Essential Books, 1959. 256p. $6.00.

> This volume of eleven chapters gives a vivid and penetrating analysis of the developments in Russia from 1861 to the opening of the revolution of 1917. The style is compact and lucid, even artistic. The content of the volume is interpretative rather than factual, and yet it is full of substance. This is

probably the best single-volume account of the period under consideration.

JMH, Vol. 31, No. 4, pp. 380-81.
R: Victor L. Albjerg

43. CURTISS, John Shelton. The Russian Revolutions of 1917. Princeton, N.J. Van Nostrand, 1957. 192p. $1.45. (Anvil Originals, No. 16)

As background to the tensions that produced the revolutions, the author sketches Russia's major unsolved problems from the Emancipation of 1861 down to 1905, with special attention given the Duma period and Russia's role in World War I. High school rather than advanced college students will profit from this narrative.

SR, Vol. 16, No. 3, p. 392.
R: Ralph T. Fisher, Jr.

44. DANIELS, Robert V. Russia. Englewood Cliffs, N.J., Prentice-Hall, 1965. 152p. $4.95, cloth; $1.95, paper.

This book presents a short summary of the main political features of the Soviet Union today, with an outline of Russian nineteenth-century history, an account of the revolutionar movement and the upheaval of 1917. The unifying theme is the view that the Soviet Union is largely a modern version of tsarist Russia, especially since Soviet totalitarianism is a direct outgrowth of the highly centralized tsarist autocracy. Useful as supplementary reading in introductory history courses or as textbook for high school instruction.

JMH, Vol. 38, No. 4, p. 423.
R: Rex A. Wade

45. DMYTRYSHYN, Basil. ed. Imperial Russia: A Source Book, 1700-1917. New York, Holt, Rinehart

& Winston, 1967. 512p. $4.95, paper.

> A collection of primary source selections, arranged chronologically, dealing with the political, social, economic, and cultural life of Imperial Russia. Many documents in the collection appear in English for the first time: official decrees, proclamations, instructions, treaties, memoirs, and political programs.

46. FLORINSKY, Michael T. The End of the Russian Empire. New York, Collier Books, 1961. 254p. $1.50, paper.

> A documentary analysis of the forces behind the 1917 Revolution and the formation of the Soviet state. Thought-provoking reading in the course of Russian history for the advanced undergraduate.

47. FRANKLAND, Noble. Imperial Tragedy: Nicholas II, Last of the Tsars. New York, Coward-MacCann, 1961. 193p. $3.95.

> Author repeats in popular fashion the story of the decline and fall of the last of the Romanovs. The various parts of the account are skillfully assembled and the book is engagingly written. Light reading for secondary school students.
>
> SR, Vol. 21, No. 1, p. 161.
> R: Martin Kilcoyne

48. GREY, Ian. Catherine the Great: Autocrat and Empress of All Russia. Philadelphia-New York, Lippincott, 1962. 254p. $6.00.

> Biography of Catherine II which includes such matters as foreign affairs, economics, and intellectual and social life. The content of the book is absorbing and can be adapted to high school use.

SR, Vol. 22, No. 1, pp. 141-42.
R: Hans Rogger

49.   HARCAVE, Sidney. First Blood: The Russian
Revolution of 1905. New York, Macmillan, 1964.
316p. $5.75.

> This excellent study exploits primary sources
> which the Soviet government has released in
> recent years. Concise summaries of the
> main currents of development toward revo-
> lution through 1904 precede a detailed exami-
> nation of four phases of the revolution. The
> appendix contains translations of official
> documents, political programs of the opposition
> parties and of the petition of Father Gapon
> which he intended to submit to the tsar on Jan-
> uary 9.

> AHR, Vol. 70, No. 4, pp. 1109-10.
> R: Arthur E. Adams

50.   HOUGH, Richard. The Potemkin Mutiny. New
York, Pantheon. 1961. 190p. $3.95.

> Skillful agitation on the part of revolutionary
> leaders among the crew and bungling by some
> of the officers led to mutiny on the cruiser
> Potemkin in 1905. This book provides good
> insight into this episode and should be wel-
> comed by any reader who is interested in the
> history of the Russian revolution and the
> history of Russia in general.

> SR, Vol. 21, No. 1, pp. 161-62.
> R: Victor P. Petrov

51.   KARPOVICH, Michael. Imperial Russia (1801-
1917). Magnolia, Mass. Peter Smith, 1932.
(1964 printing) 114p. $2.50, paper.

> Condensed discussion of Russian history of
> the nineteenth century, emphasizing reforms
> after 1855. Still useful for beginning students
> of Russian history.

52. KLIUCHEVSKY, Vasili. <u>Peter the Great</u>. Trans-
     lated by Liliana Archibald. New York, St. Mar-
     tin's Press, 1958. 282p. $7.50.

>   Still the best standard work on Peter I.
>   Soviet scholars have found it worthy of two
>   reprints. The translator furnishes excep-
>   tionally apt references to recent Western
>   books and essays on Peter's era. This
>   valuable volume deserves a place in
>   educational libraries.
>
>   SR, Vol. 22, No. 1, pp. 140-41.
>   R: Albert Parry

53. KOHN, Hans. <u>Basic History of Modern Russia</u>:
     Political, Cultural and Social Trends. Princeton,
     N. J., Van Nostrand, 1957. 192p. $1.45. (Anvil
     Originals, No. 24)

>   A brief history of Russia in the nineteenth
>   century. This short study should be useful
>   to high school students.
>
>   SR, Vol. 17, No. 2, p. 235.
>   R: Robert F. Byrnes

54. LENSEN, George Alexander. ed. <u>Russia's Eastward</u>
     <u>Expansion</u>. Englewood Cliffs, N. J., Prentice-Hall,
     1964. 184p. $4.50, cloth; $1.95 paper.

>   Collection of readings of Russian and West-
>   ern authors on Russian expansion into Cen-
>   tral Asia, Siberia and the Far East since
>   the Middle Ages. Six maps and a bibliog-
>   raphy accompany this interesting reader.

55. MASSIE, Robert K. <u>Nicholas and Alexandra</u>. New
     York, Atheneum, 1967 613p. $7.50.

>   The story of the Russian Imperial family;
>   their fall from the pinnacle of power to im-
>   prisonment and death. This lively narrative
>   can be recommended to high school students.

56.　MAZOUR, Anatole G.　Rise and Fall of the Romanovs.
Princeton, N. J., Van Nostrand, 1960.　192p.　$1.45.
(Anvil Originals, No. 50)

> Provided is a key to Russia's development
> from the accession to the throne of the first
> of the Romanovs in 1613 to the assassination
> of Russia's last tsar in 1917.　The book illus-
> trates how strongly the Romanovs influenced
> the course of modern European history by
> dictating Russia's foreign policy.　A beginner
> will appreciate this study for its clarity and
> brevity.
>
> SEER, Vol. 49, No. 93, p. 570.
> R: J. L. H. Keep

57.　McKENZIE, Walter P.　Russian Economic Policy
Under Nicholas I.　Ithaca, N. Y., Cornell University
Press, 1967.　320p.　$8.75.

> During the second quarter of the nineteenth
> century, Russia's position as a major Euro-
> pean power gradually declined and was final-
> ly dealt a shattering blow by the Crimean
> War.　This book deals exclusively with
> economic policy and its contribution to the
> decline.　The author unravels the complicated
> reasons for the failure of Russian economic
> policy.

58.　MOSSE, Werner E.　Alexander II and the Modernization of Russia.　Rev. ed.　New York, Macmillan,
1958.　191p.　$2.50; New York, Collier Books,
1962.　191p.　$1.25, paper.

> A well-informed, intelligent and perceptive
> account of the reign of Alexander II (1855-1881).
> A combined scholarship and popularization
> has been achieved by the author.　The tsar
> reformer and tsar despot in one person, as
> presented in this volume, belongs to the most
> important figures in Russian history.

AHR, Vol. 65, No. 1, p. 180.
R: Nicholas V. Riasanovsky

59. PIERCE, Richard A. Russian Central Asia 1867-1917: A Study in Colonial Rule. Berkeley, University of California Press, 1960. 359p. $7.00.

> It is widely believed in Europe and America that Russia is "untainted by the sin of colonialism, " that she never had and does not have a subject empire. This study proves otherwise. A revealing account of Russian imperialism which has long been needed.

> SEER, Vol. 49, No. 93, pp. 547-48.
> R: H. Seton-Watson

60. PUSHKAREV, Sergei. The Emergence of Modern Russia, 1801-1917. Translated from Russian by Robert H. MacNeal and Tova Yedlin. New York, Holt, Rinehart & Winston, 1963. 512p. $8.75.

> A Russian national historian discusses Russia's political structure, her foreign relations, social and economic conditions and her cultural history.

61. RAEFF, Marc. The Decembrist Movement. Englewood Cliffs, N.J., Prentice-Hall, 1966. 180p. $2.95, paper. (Russian Civilization Series, edited by Michael Cherniavsky and Ivo J. Lederer)

> The author examines the factors that contributed to the December rebellion against the ascendance to the throne of Nicholas I with all their political, social and economic impacts.

62. RAEFF, Marc. ed. Plans for Political Reform in Imperial Russia, 1730-1905. Englewood Cliffs, N.J., Prentice-Hall, 1966. 159p. $4.95, cloth; $2.95, paper. (Russian Civilization Series, edited by Michael Cherniavsky and Ivo J. Lederer)

Translation of selected primary sources re-
lating to a particular problem in Russian
history. The documents are in unabridged
form, wherever feasible, and are succinctly
annotated. Each volume of the Russian
Civilization Series has a brief critical
bibliography and an introductory essay by
the compiler. Useful as supplementary
reader.

SEER, Vol. 45, No. 104, pp. 251-53.
R: John Keep

63. RAEFF, Marc. ed. Peter the Great: Reformer or
Revolutionary? Boston, Heath, 1966. 109p. $1.50.
(Problems in European Civilization)

Selection of articles with an introduction that
not only sets Peter's reforms in the pertinent
Russian and European background, but also
includes an interpretation of Peter I, that is
significant in its own right. This volume can
be suggested for all courses dealing with 18th
century Russian history, as well as for a
specific study of Peter the Great.

CSS, Vol. 1, No. 1, pp. 130-31.
R: Andrew Ezergailis

64. RIASANOVSKY, Nicholas V. Nicholas I and Official
Nationality in Russia 1825-1855. Berkeley, University of California Press, 1959. 296p. $6.50, cloth;
$1.95, paper.

General survey of the policies of Nicholas I,
with special emphasis on the doctrine of
official nationality, which, together with
Orthodoxy and autocracy, formed the famous
threefold slogan of Count Uvarov. Rewarding for the student who lacks knowledge of
Russian.

SEER, Vol. 39, No. 92, pp. 259-61.
R: H. Seton-Watson

65. ROGGER, Hans J. National Consciousness in
Eighteenth Century Russia. Cambridge, Harvard
University Press, 1960. 391p. $6.75.

> Original study of the growth of Russian
> national consciousness based on the best
> available sources. Relevant to the study of
> Russian cultural and political development
> during the eighteenth century. Suitable for
> advanced students of Russian history.

> SR, Vol. 20, No. 2, p. 321-23.
> R: Alexander Lipski

66. SCHWARZ, Solomon M. The History of Menshevism.
Vol. I: The Russian Revolution of 1905; The Workers'
Movement and the Formation of Bolshevism and
Menshevism. Chicago, University of Chicago Press,
1967. 361p. $8.95. (Hoover Institution Publications)

> This book covers the crucial period during
> 1905 when Social-Democracy emerged as a
> factor of consequence on the political scene,
> only to divide into the two parts that became
> Social-Democracy, on the one hand, and,
> on the other, the authoritarian labor move-
> ment that assumed the name of Communism.
> The author was a member of the Kerensky
> government.

67. SETON-WATSON, Hugh. The Decline of Imperial
Russia, 1855-1914. New York, Praeger, 1962.
406p. $7.50, cloth; $2.95, paper.

> This study aims at explaining the stages of
> the decline of Russian tsardom between the
> Crimean War and World War I. This book
> is an example of objectivity, balance and
> clarity of presentation.

> SR, Vol. 12, No. 3, pp. 396-98.
> R: D. von Mohrenschildt

68. SETON-WATSON, Hugh. The Russian Empire, 1801-1917. New York, Oxford University Press, 1967. 750p. $10.00.

> The most comprehensive history of nineteenth century Russia, containing a profusion of facts about Russian political history. Seventeen maps and a splendid bibliography enhance this lucid study. College libraries must not overlook this title.

69. SUMNER, Benedict H. Peter the Great and the Emergence of Russia. New York, Macmillan, 1951. 216p. $2.00; New York, Collier Books, 1956. 216p. $0.95, paper.

> Short discussion of Peter's reign, his foreign relations and reforms in particular. The author has only praise for this unusual Russian autocratic ruler.
>
> SR, Vol. 12, No. 1, pp. 144-45.
> R: C. E. Black

70. VON LAUE, Theodore H. Sergei Witte and the Industrialization of Russia. New York, London, Columbia University Press, 1963. 360p. $7.50. (Studies of the Russian Institute, Columbia University)

> An admirable work on some crucial aspects in the life and career of the man who, theoretically speaking, could have altered the course of Russia's development. This book is a valuable contribution by Western scholarship to the study of modern Russian history and includes a comprehensive bibliography. A welcome title to the list of suggested reading for advanced students.
>
> SR, Vol. 24, No. 2, pp. 325-27.
> R: Arcadius Kahan

71. WOODWARD, David. The Russians at Sea: A History of the Russian Navy. New York, Praeger, 1966. 254p. $6.95.

> The author offers an absorbing account of the Russian navy from its meager beginnings under Peter I, to its current position of power. He also examines the role this navy played in the past. This study aids in understanding Russian expansion on land and on sea.

K. Foreign Relations

72. ENTNER, Marvin L. Russo-Persian Commercial Relations, 1828-1914. Gainesville, University of Florida Press, 1965. 80p. $2.00. (University of Florida Monographs, Social Sciences, No. 28)

> This gracious little monograph explains successfully the nature of Russian commercial penetration and the methods of economic exploitation of Persia.

> AHR, Vol. 71, No. 4, pp. 1292-93.
> R: C. M. Foust

73. JELAVICH, Barbara. A Century of Russian Foreign Policy 1814-1914. Philadelphia-New York, Lippincott, 1964. 308p. $4.50, cloth; $1.80, paper. (The Lippincott History Series)

> A useful survey of Russian foreign policy in the nineteenth century. Stressed throughout are questions of ideology and national interest. A valuable addition to the understanding of Russia's behavior in the area of foreign policy. Recommended for advanced undergraduates.

> SEER, Vol. 18, No. 101, p. 492.
> R: B. Hollingsworth

74.   JELAVICH, Charles. Tsarist Russia and Balkan Nationalism: Russian Influence in the International Affairs of Bulgaria and Serbia, 1879-1886. Berkeley, University of California Press, 1958. 304p. $6.50.

> The author discusses the influence of military consideration on the formulation of Russian policy. The study sheds light on the motives of Russian engagement in Bulgaria and Serbia.

> SEER, Vol. 39, No. 92, pp. 263-65.
> R: W. N. Medilicott

75.   LAQUEUR, Walter. Russia and Germany: A Century of Conflict. Boston, Little, Brown & Co. 1965. 367p. $6.75, cloth; $2.65, paper.

> This is not predominantly diplomatic history, but rather a history of the ideas and attitudes of certain circles that profoundly affected the relationship and history of the two countries. The author deals with the metapolitics of Russian-German relations, in particular with specific Russian influences on Nazi ideology; hence, it is a history of ideas and intellectual relations, with political, economic and military developments placed in their proper context.

> AHR, Vol. 71, No. 4, pp. 1323-24.
> R: Carl G. Anthon

76.   MOSSE, Werner E. The Rise and Fall of the Crimean System, 1855-71: The Story of a Peace Settlement. New York, St. Martin's Press, 1963. 213p. $8.00.

> A critical account of events which led to the Treaty of 1856 and of the subsequent Russian efforts to revise the provisions of this settlement. An excellent case study of Russian foreign policy under Alexander II.

AHR, Vol. 69, No. 4, p. 1132.
R: Dwight E. Lee

77.   OLIVA, L. Jay. ed. <u>Russia and the West</u>: From
Peter to Khrushchev. Boston, Heath, 1965. 289p.
$6.50, cloth; $2.50, paper. (D.C. Heath Studies
in History and Politics)

> Collection of excerpts from the writings of
> those who have described important aspects
> of the process of Russia's Westernization, or
> interpreted its manifestations. Included are
> observations of ministers of state, foreign
> ambassadors and historians. The political
> and diplomatic relations of Russia and the
> West are given equal weight with the cultural
> and the intellectual. A very useful volume
> for students lacking knowledge of Russian.

> CSS, Vol. 1, No. 1, pp. 148-49.
> R: Charles C. Adler, Jr.

78.   SMITH, Clarence Jay. <u>The Russian Struggle For
Power, 1914-1917</u>: A Study of Russian Foreign
Policy During the First World War. New York,
Philosophical Library, 1956. 553p. $4.75.

> The author, using Russian original documents,
> produced the first integrated and detailed
> account of tsarist diplomacy during the war.
> This study still has practical value despite
> its mechanical approach and should be con-
> sulted together with those published more
> recently.

79.   WILLIAMS, William A. <u>American-Russian Relations 1781-1947</u>. New York, Rinehart, 1952.
367p. $5.00.

> This book deals chiefly with the American
> policy toward Russia during World War I,
> the Revolution and thereafter. This study
> is indispensable for the student of American-

Russian affairs during the early years of the Revolution.

SR, Vol. 12, No. 3, pp. 392-94.
R: E. H. Carr

L. Politics and Government

80.   ANDERSON, Thornton. Russian Political Thought: An Introduction. Ithaca, N. Y., Cornell University Press, 1967. 432p. $9.75.

An appraisal of Russian political theory and practice. The author examines the present Soviet regime, not simply in terms of its Marxist-Leninist concepts, but as a development of traditional Russian political assumptions. He shows how Orthodoxy, Mongol invasions, the fall of Byzantium, and even attempts at Westernization under Peter and Catherine led to the present isolation of Russia from the West. Students of political science will find many answers in this penetrating study.

81.   MARX, Karl and Friederich Engels. The Russian Menace to Europe. Edited by Paul W. Blackstock and Bert F. Hoselitz. New York, The Free Press, 1952. 288p. $4.95.

It is not surprising that both founding fathers of Marxism were extremely anti-Russian. Marx and Engels were well aware of Russian expansionism as this collection of their writings amply proves. Reading of this unusual work will stimulate class discussion.

82.   RAEFF, Marc. Michael Speransky: Statesman of Imperial Russia, 1772-1839. The Hague, Nijhoff, 1957. 387p. Guilders 27.50.

This book offers a wealth of facts, opinions, and interpretations. It deals with the constitutional plans in the reign of Alexander I, the nature and organization and bureaucracy and the codification of law at the time of Nicholas I. Speransky's role is well described. An extensive bibliography contributes to the lasting value of this book.

JMH, Vol. 30, No. 3, pp. 291-92.
R: Nicholas V. Riasanovsky

83.   RAEFF, Marc. Plans for Political Reform in Imperial Russia, 1730-1905. (See entry No. 62)

84.   THADEN, Edward C. Conservative Nationalism in Nineteenth-Century Russia. Seattle, University of Washington Press, 1964. 271p. $9.50.

This comprehensive, erudite and lucid study of the Russian conservative thought in the last century is an important contribution to an understanding of Russian social and intellectual thought. Slavophilism and official nationalism are also analyzed. A worthwhile additional reading material.

JMH, Vol. 37, No. 4, pp. 489-90.
R: Alfred Levin

85.   UTECHIN, Sergej V. Russian Political Thought: A Concise History. New York, Praeger, 1963. 320p. $2.25, paper.

A brief history of Russian political thought from medieval Russia to Communism and revolutionary anti-Communism. Discussion of all major cultural and political movements and their leaders. Important contribution to the study of social and intellectual history of Russia.

86.   WALKIN, Jacob.   The Rise of Democracy in Pre-
      Revolutionary Russia: Political and Social Institu-
      tions Under the Last Three Czars.   New York,
      Praeger, 1962.   320p. $6.50 (Praeger Publica-
      tions in Russian History and World Communism,
      No. 115).

> Informative and interesting treatment of
> pre-revolutionary development in Russia.
> Highly recommended to those specifically
> interested in its subject as well as the
> general reader.
>
> AHR, Vol. 68, No. 4, pp. 1062-63.
> R: Nicholas V. Riasanovsky

M.   Social and Intellectual History

87.   AVRICH, Paul.   The Russian Anarchists.   Princeton,
      Princeton University Press, 1967.   303p. $7.50.
      (Studies of the Russian Institute, Columbia Univers-
      ity)

> The author records the history of the anarchist
> movement from its Russian origins in the
> nineteenth century, with a discussion of
> Bakunin and Kropotkin, to its upsurge in the
> 1905 and 1917 revolutions and its fall under
> the Bolshevik regime.

88.   BILL, Valentine T.   The Forgotten Class: The
      Russian Bourgeoisie From the Earliest Beginnings
      to 1900.   New York, Praeger, 1959.   229p.
      $5.00.

> A history of the industrial and commercial
> establishment in Russia which, by accept-
> ing the idea of Russia's Westernization,
> sought to modernize that country through
> the changes in social and economic struc-
> tures.   The book also analyzes the causes

of their final failure in 1917. Recommended for students of Russian history of the nineteenth century.

89. BILLINGTON, James H. The Icon and the Axe: An Interpretive History of Six Centuries of Russian Thought and Culture. New York, Knopf, 1966. 786p. $15.00.

> This volume represents one of the most significant books on Russia that has appeared since World War II. A major addition to Western understanding of the wellsprings of Russian spirit, synonymous with Soviet spirit. The book will jolt its readers out of the intellectual torpor induced by the standard English-language surveys. An inspiring work that must not be ignored by instructor and student alike.

> SR, Vol. 26, No. 1, pp. 117-27.
> R: George D. Jackson, Jr.

90. BILLINGTON, James H. Mikhailovsky and Russian Populism. London, Clarendon Press, 1956. 217p. $4.80.

> This study illuminates in detail a period often obscured between the revolutionary radicalism of the 1860's and the growing Marxism of the late 1890's. Mikhailovsky is taken as the symbol and the very personification of the populist hopes of the era and the eventual disillusionment which continous failure gave rise to. A valuable addition to the growing library on Russian intellectual history.

> SR, Vol. 18, No. 2, pp. 264-65.
> R: Miriam Haskell Berlin

91. BLUM, Jerome. Lord and Peasant in Russia: From the Ninth to the Nineteenth Century. Princeton, Princeton University Press, 1961. 656p. $12.50.

Against the background of Russian political
and economic evolution, the author traces
the history of the lords and peasants, and
the relationship between them. He also
elaborates on the emancipation of the serfs
in 1861. An outstanding work from which
the advanced student will gain many insights.

SEEJ, Vol. 12, No. 2, pp. 220-21.
R: Oswald P. Backus

92. CHERNIAVSKY, Michael. Tsar and People: Studies
in Russian Myths. New Haven, Yale University
Press, 1961. 258p. $6.00.

Original study in Russian mythology trying
to explain the thinking of Russian people in
their relationship to the church, tsars, and
state, in view of the notion of "Holy Russia."
Helpful for the study of the Russian mentality
and its culture. Because of the nature of the
material this work is not recommended for
secondary school use, however, an alert
instructor might profit greatly by it in pre-
paring an attractive lecture on the "Russian
soul."

SR, Vol. 21, No. 2, pp. 344-46.
R: Marc Raeff

93. FADNER, Frank. Seventy Years of Pan-Slavism
in Russia: Karamzin to Danilevskii, 1800-1870.
Washington, Georgetown University Press,
1962. 429p. $7.50, cloth; $6.00, paper.

The author has presented a survey of nineteenth-century Russian nationalism known
as Pan-Slavism. To some degree, it is
a scholarly handbook of Pan-Slavism, with
the author providing pertinent biographical
data for each prominent figure, summarizing
that person's view and analyzing his particular contribution to Pan-Slavic thought. This

is a solid, well-documented study which
deserves its place in any college library.

SEEJ, Vol. 8, No. 1, pp. 99-100.
R: Horace W. Dewey

94.   FISCHER, George. Russian Liberalism From
Gentry to Intelligentsia. Cambridge, Harvard
University Press, 1958. 240p. $4.50. (Russian
Research Center Studies, No. 30)

> The author draws a picture of transition from
> the localized impulse for reform among the
> gentry under Alexander II to the more general-
> ized and radical reformism of the generation
> of "grandsons" at the turn of the century.
> He relates this development to the emergence
> of a professional middle class in Russia,
> suggests frequent parallels with the problems
> of liberal reformers in underdeveloped
> countries, and adds a full and valuable
> critical bibliography.

> SR, Vol. 19, No. 2, pp. 289-91.
> R: James H. Billington

95.   HECHT, David. Russian Radicals Look to America
1825-1894. Cambridge, Harvard University Press,
(1947) 251p. $4.00.

> The author has attempted to analyze the
> "impact of American institutional experience
> and example upon a numerically small, but
> especially significant group of two genera-
> tions of pre-Marxian revolutionaries." He
> graphically traces the transformation of
> the Russian radicals' attitude toward
> America. Such figures as Herzen, Ogarev,
> Bakunin, Chernyshevsky, Chaikovsky and
> Lavrov are dealt with.

> SR, Vol. 7, No. 1, pp. 94-95.
> R: Paul H. Aron

96. HERTZEN, Aleksandr I. From the Other Shore, and The Russian People and Socialism, an Open Letter to Jules Michelet. Introduction by Isaiach Berlin. New York, Braziller, 1956. 208p. $3.75.

> The editor of "The Bell" in London addresses himself to Russia's social and political conditions of the middle of the nineteenth century. Hertzen's writings became an essential part of Russian liberal and socialist tradition.

97. KOHN, Hans. ed. The Mind of Modern Russia: Historical and Political Thought of Russia's Great Age. New Brunswick, N.J. Rutgers University Press, 1955. 298p. $5.50.

> This book covers the period from the end of the Napoleonic wars to the First World War. The editor offers excerpts from writings of Chadaev, Pogodin, Tjuchev, Khomjakov, Aksakov, Herzen, Danilevskij, Solovev, Lenin Berdjaev, among others. In this way, representatives of all major philosophies came to word. The selection is still useful for addition reading on all levels of Russian studies.

> SR, Vol. 16, No. 3, pp. 416-19.
> R: John Somerville

98. LAMPERT, Eugene. Sons Against Fathers: Studies in Russian Radicalism and Revolution. New York, Oxford University Press, 1964. 405p. $10.10.

> This is a lively, provocative book; both scholarly and entertaining, it is one of the most readable and at the same time one of the most richly suggestive books on the history of nineteenth-century Russia. Chernyshevsky, Dobroliubov, and Pisarev are treated in this study. An excellent supplement to textbooks on Russian history.

> SR, Vol. 24, No. 4, pp. 725-26.
> R: Sidney Monas

99. LAMPERT, Eugene. Studies in Rebellion: Belinsky-Bakunin-Herzen. New York, Praeger, 1957. 295p. $6.00.

> The author emphasizes their irrational instincts, the duality of their nature, their desire "to transform every issue into high metaphysics." He also stresses the contradictions existing outside human personalities in the life of a nation and in the historical process, which affect man. Lengthy quotations from the writings of these rebels show their inconsistencies and their changing attitudes. The study adds its share to the history of Russian thought.
>
> JMH, Vol. 30, No. 4, pp. 371-72.
> R: Walther Kirchner

100. LANG, David M. The First Russian Radical: Alexander Radishchev, 1749-1802. London, Allen & Unwin, 1959. 208p. $8.00.

> A new interpretation of the life and work of Radishchev is presented in this study. It sheds new light on Russia's social and political institutions in the late eighteenth century under Catherine II.

100a. LAVROV, Peter. Historical Letters Peter Lavrov. Translated, with introduction and notes, by James P. Scanlan. Berkeley, University of California Press, 1967.

> Lavrov's Historical Letters contain the first discussion in the legal Russian press of the principles of militant party action later elaborated by Lenin and the Russian Communists. This volume is a translation of the so-called "Paris edition" of the Letters.

101. LUKASHEVICH, Stephen. Ivan Aksakov, 1823-1886: A Study in Russian Thought and Politics. Cambridge,

Harvard University Press, 1965. 191p. $5.50.
(Harvard Historical Monugraphes, No. 57)

> The study is not only the first and only com-
> plete biography of Aksakov, one of the pillars
> of Slavophilism, it is also an impressively
> concise and lucid exposition of the ideology
> of that movement as a whole. The book's
> appeal to the student of history and politics
> is self-evident. It is singularly well written
> and makes fascinating reading.
>
> SEEJ, Vol. 11, No. 1, pp. 95-96.
> R: Maurice Friedberg

102. McCONNELL, Allen. A Russian Philosophe:
Alexander Radishchev, 1749-1802. The Hague,
Nijhoff, 1964. 228p. Guilders 24.25.

> Radishchev occupies a prominent place in
> the history of Russian liberal thought. His
> Journey from St. Petersburg to Moscow
> constitutes a most devastating indictment of
> the Russian ancien regime. Serfdom and
> administrative corruption were attacked
> most savagely.
>
> AHR, Vol. 70, No. 4, pp. 1204-05.
> R: Anatole G. Mazour

103. MALIA, Martin. Alexander Herzen and the Birth of
Russian Socialism, 1812-1855. Cambridge, Harvard
University Press, 1961. New York, Grosset &
Dunlap, 1965. 486p. $10.00, cloth; $2.65, paper.
(Russian Research Center Studies, No. 39)

> A careful analysis of the thought of this most
> characteristic Russian liberal of the middle
> of the nineteenth century. This noble thinker
> opposed Russian chauvinism concerning the
> Poles and Ukrainians. An excellent contri-
> bution to the intellectual history of Russia
> which should not be missed in a library col-
> lection.

AHR, Vol. 67, No. 3, pp. 723-24.
R: Hans Kohn

104. MAZOUR, Anatole G. The First Russian Revolution, 1825: The Decembrist Movement. Its Origins, Development, and Significance. Berkeley, University of California Press, 1937. 324p. $7.50, cloth; Reprint: Stanford University Press, 1965. 328p. $2.95, paper.

> A detailed treatise on Decembrist movements. This volume is an important contribution to our understanding of Russian history of the nineteenth century. It still remains the classic work on this topic in the English language.

> SEER, Vol. 45, No. 105, pp. 558-59.
> R: Barry Hollingworth

105. PAYNE, Robert. The Terrorists: The Story of the Forerunners of Stalin. New York, Funk & Wagnalls, 1957. 381p. $5.00.

> The story tells of the four revolutionaries, Nechayev, Zhelyabov, Sazonov and Kaliayev, who engaged in terrorist activities under the last three tsars. The author used contemporary sources to reproduce this little known aspect of Russian history.

106. PETROVICH, Michael B. The Emergence of Russian Panslavism, 1856-1870. New York, Columbia University Press, 1956. 312p. $5.00. (Studies of the Russian Institute, Columbia University)

> The author examines the origin and the ideology of Russian Panslavism which became an instrument in Russian policy during the second half of the last and the early years of this century. This thought-provoking work provides profitable reading for the student.

> JMH, Vol. 39, No. 4, p. 388.
> R: Leonid I. Strakhovsky

107.   PIPES, Richard. ed. The Russian Intelligentsia.
New York, Columbia University Press, 1961.   234p.
$6.00.

> A collection of essays dealing with the Russian
> intelligentsia.   While this volume does not
> clarify the complex state of affairs, it contri-
> butes considerably to a better understanding of
> the social composition of the intellectuals.
>
> JMH, Vol. 33, No. 4, p. 472.
> R: Anatole G. Mazour

108.   PYZIUR, Eugene.   The Doctrine of Anarchism of
Michael A. Bakunin.   Milwaukee, Marquette Univers-
ity Press, 1955.   158p. $4.20.   (Marquette Slavic
Studies, No. 1)

> Critical evaluation of Bakunin's thought.   The
> author sees Bakunin's personality as the
> mainspring of his thought and action and
> attributes to external factors only a secondary
> significance.
>
> SR, Vol. 16, No. 4, pp. 551-52.
> R: Samuel H. Baron

109.   RADISHCHEV, Aleksandr N.   A Journey from St.
Petersburg to Moscow.   Translated by Leo Wiener;
edited by Roderick Page Thaler.   Cambridge,
Harvard University Press, 1958.   286p. $6.50.

> This is the first translation of Radishchev's
> memoirs into English in which he attacked
> serfdom and autocracy in 1790.   Catherine
> immediately directed that all copies be
> collected and burned.   She saw in the Journey
> a criminal and revolutionary work.   This
> account should be thoroughly studied in
> colleges.
>
> SR, Vol. 19, No. 1, pp. 108-9.
> R: Allen McConnell

110. RAEFF, Marc. Origins of the Russian Intelligentsia:
The Eighteenth Century Nobility. New York, Harcourt,
Brace & World, 1967. 256p. $2.45, paper.

> The volume offers an investigation and analysis
> of the leadership group from which the revolu-
> tionary nineteenth-century Russian intelligentsia
> emerged. It furthermore examines the institu-
> tional and intellectual experiences of the Russian
> nobility in the eighteenth century. A pioneering
> study on this aspect of Russian history.

111. RAEFF, Marc. ed. Russian Intellectual History: An
Anthology. Introduction by Isaiah Berlin. New York,
Harcourt, Brace & World, 1966. 404p. $4.95,
paper. (The Harbrace Series in Russian Area Studies)

> Selection of short articles and essays intended
> to acquaint the English-speaking student with
> the social and political consciousness of modern
> Russia. Most of these documents of the eight-
> eenth- and nineteenth-century intelligentsia
> have never before appeared in English trans-
> lation. Karamzin, Chadaev, Kireevski,
> Khomiakov, and Tolstoy are among the con-
> tributors.

112. RIASANOVSKY, Nicholas V. Russia and the West in
the Teaching of the Slavophils. Cambridge, Harvard
University Press, 1952. 244p. $5.00.

> This book provides the student with a well-
> documented summary of the thought of six
> leading Slavophils, together with an apprecia-
> tion of the part which they plays in forming a
> Europeanized Russian intelligentsia in the
> nineteenth century. The text is carefully
> annotated, and the ample bibliography is
> of special value for further reading and
> research.
>
> SR, Vol. 13, No. 3, pp. 441-42.
> R: Richard Hare

112a.   ROBINSON, Geroid Tanquary. <u>Rural Russia Under
        the Old Regime.</u> Berkeley, University of California
        Press, 1967. 342p. $1.95, paper (reissue)

> The author makes clear the role played by
> the Russian peasant in the development of
> the forces of revolution, and how the emanci-
> pation of 1861 and the agrarian revolution of
> 1905 contributed to the decline of rural societ
> in old Russia.

112b.   SCHAPIRO, Leonard. <u>Rationalism and Nationalism
        in Russian Nineteenth-Century Political Thought.</u>
        New Haven, Yale University Press, 1967. 184p.
        $5.00. (Yale Russian and East European Series,
        No. 4)

> The author portraits rationalists as the fol-
> lowers of Europe and nationalists as Rus-
> sian isolationists. He examines both tradi-
> tions, including the writing and influence of
> such figures as Speransky, Berdiaev, Chaada
> Pushkin, and Pestel.

113.   TOMPKINS, Stuart Ramsay. <u>The Russian Intelli-
        gentsia:</u> Makers of the Revolutionary State. Norman,
        University of Oklahoma Press, 1957. 282p. $5.00.

> A discussion of the radical and intellectual
> currents of the nineteenth and early twentieth
> century; Nihilism, Populism, the Marxists
> and Social Revolutionaries. The study con-
> veys a deeper understanding of the causes of
> the Bolshevik revolution.

114.   TOMPKINS, Stuart Ramsay. <u>The Russian Mind.</u>
        Vol. I: From Peter the Great Through the En-
        lightenment. Norman, University of Oklahoma
        Press, 1953. 302p. $4.00.

> Cultural and intellectual aspects such as
> classes, education, press, censorship and
> Free Masonry are treated in this topic. The
> author traces the degree of continuity between

Tsarist Russia and its successor, the Soviet
Union. Recommended for courses in Russian history to help clarify differences between East and West.

115. VENTURI, Franco. Roots of Revolution: A History
of the Populist and Socialist Movements in Nineteenth-Century Russia. Translated by Frances Haskell.
New York, Knopf, 1961. 850p. $12.75; New York,
Grosset & Dunlap, 1966. $3.45, paper.

> Detailed study of social and intellectual
> nineteenth-century Russian history. Challenging reading, though a good background
> in general Russian history is necessary to
> follow the author's presentation.

> SR, Vol. 20, No. 4, pp. 710-12.
> R: Joseph Frank

115a. VUCINICH, Wayne S. ed. The Peasant in Nineteenth-Century Russia. Stanford, Stanford University Press,
1967. 320p. $8.50.

> The eight studies collected in this volume
> comprise the picture of the nineteenth-century
> Russian peasantry. They also demonstrate
> the centrality of the peasant in the entire
> institutional and cultural history of Russia.

116. YARMOLINSKY, Avrahm. Road to Revolution:
A Century of Russian Radicalism. London, Cassell,
1957. 369p. 25s; New York, Macmillan, 1959.
349p. $5.95; Collier Books, 1962. $1.50, paper.

> This is a history of the Russian revolutionary
> movement of the nineteenth century that
> brings pleasure and enlightenment to the
> nonspecialist reader; it also makes useful
> additional reading in courses on modern
> Russian history. An indispensable volume
> for the study of Russian political and social
> thought.

AHR, Vol. 64, No. 1, p. 1065.
R: Martin Malia

N. Marxism and Communism in Russia

(See also chapter on Communism)

117.   BARON, Samuel H. Plekhanov: The Father of Russian Marxism. Stanford, Stanford University Press, 1963. 400p. $8.50, cloth; $2.95, paper.

> The author is the leading American expert on Plekhanov who has studied the life and work of this noted Russian Marxist since the late 1940's which is reflected in this excellent piece of scholarship.

> SEEJ, Vol. 8, No. 4, pp. 476-77.
> R: Edward C. Thaden

118.   BERDIAEV, Nikolai A. Origin of Russian Communis Ann Arbor, University of Michigan Press, 1960. 19**1** $1.65.

> As a well-known Russian philosopher and educator, the author interprets the paramute question of the origin of Bolshevism in Russia. Significantly, he sees more causes in the Russian past than Soviet historians are willing to admit. Bolshevism is a symbol of Russian intellectual and spiritual disease. Students should be encouraged to get acquainted with Berdiaev's point of view.

118a.   DeGEORGE, Richard T. Patterns of Soviet Thought: The Origins and Development of Dialectical and Historical Materialism. Ann Arbor, University of Michigan Press, 1966. 293p. $6.95.

> This book summarizes and gives a detailed critique of the basic works of Marxist-Lenini philosophy from its German origins to its

latest developments in the Soviet Union. It is also a case study of Soviet philosophy.

SR, Vol. 26, No. 4, pp. 695-96.
R: David D. Comey

119. HAIMSON, Leopold H. The Russian Marxists and the Origin of Bolshevism. Cambridge, Harvard University Press, 1955. 246p. $6.00. (Russian Research Center Studies, No. 19)

Examination of the earliest period of Russian Marxism, from the split in the revolutionary society Land and Freedom in 1879 to the split in the Russian Social Democratic Labor (Marxist) Party in 1903, with some additional material up to January, 1905. The study focuses on four historical figures: Axelrod, Plekhanov, Martov and Lenin.

JMH, Vol. 28, No. 2, pp. 210-11.
R: Donald W. Treadgold

120. TREADGOLD, Donald W. Lenin and His Rivals: The Struggle for Russia's Future, 1898-1906. New York, Praeger, 1955. 291p. $5.00.

The book explains the failure of the opposition parties, preceding and during the 1905 revolution, to obtain liberal constituent concessions. The discussion, centering on Russian liberals and Socialist Revolutionaries, furnishes a welcome background for an understanding of events that followed in 1917 and after.

JMH, Vol. 28, No. 2, pp. 211-12.
R: Robert E. MacMaster

121. ULAM, Adam B. The Bolsheviks: The Intellectual, Personal and Political History of the Origins of Russian Communism. New York, Macmillan, 1965. 598p. $9.95.

This book is best described as a highly enriched biography of V.I. Lenin. On the other

hand, it also concerns his supporters and
opponents. The study is directed toward
the serious student of Communist affairs,
since it assumes of the reader a basic
familiarity with Russian history. The
teacher will have to get acquainted with this
masterpiece of scholarship.

JMH, Vol. 39, No. 2, pp. 204-205.
R: Francis B. Randall

O. Philosophy

122. EDIE, James M. et al. eds. Russian Philosophy.
3 vols. Vol. I: The Beginnings of Russian Philosophy; The Slavophiles; The Westernizers; Vol. II:
The Nihilists; The Populists; Critics of Religion
and Culture; Vol. III: Pre-Revolutionary Philosophy
and Theology; Philosophers in Exile; Marxists and
Communists. Chicago, Quadrangle Book, 1965.
434, 312, 521p. $7.50, $6.50, $8.50, respectively.

This important publication, the only one of
its kind in English, makes possible the
teaching of Russian philosophy and civilization. It contains 69 selections from 27 philosophers, chronologically arranged. Librarie
should not be without this informative and
pioneering work.

123. MacMASTER, Robert E. Danilevsky: A Russian
Totalitarian Philosopher. Cambridge, Harvard
University Press, 1967. 368p. $7.95. (Russian
Research Center Studies, No. 53)

The author re-examines the life and work of
Nicholas I. Danilevsky (1822-1885) who is
known for his book Russia and Europe.
Danilevsky is portrayed as a totalitarian
thinker and self-styled political prophet
whose theories bear striking resemblance
to Bolshevism.

124. ZENKOVSKY, Vasilii V. A History of Russian
Philosophy. Translated by George L. Kline. New
York, Columbia University Press, 1953. 2 Vols.
$15. 00.

> A survey of Russian philosophical thought,
> secular and religious, from the eighteenth
> to the mid-twentieth century. Adaptable as
> textbook for the history of Russian philosophy.

CHAPTER II

RSFSR-USSR, 1917 (1923) to the Present

A. Encyclopedias and Handbooks

125.   FITZSIMMONS, Thomas. ed. USSR, Its People, Its
Society, Its Culture. New York, Taplinger Publishing Co. for the Human Relations Areas Files Press,
1960. 590p. $8.50.

> Broad in coverage, this volume treats geog-
> raphy, history, government, politics, eco-
> nomics, and education, among other topics.
> An objective tone prevails throughout. It is
> useful for general reference and also for
> introduction to this particular area of
> studies.
>
> SR, Vol. 22, No. 2, pp. 349-50.
> R: Lawrence Krader

126.   FLORINSKY, Michael T. ed. McGraw-Hill Encyclopedia of Russia and the Soviet Union. New York,
McGraw-Hill, 1961. 624p. $23.50.

> A comprehensive and systematic inventory
> with unmatched coverage in depth, width
> and expertise of the contemporary status of
> our knowledge concerning the Soviet Union.
> The joint cooperative efforts of the editor
> and of more than one hundred contributors
> have yielded an excellent end product. It
> answers a number of questions that may be
> asked by the specialist and student alike.
> A particularly sound investment for a library
> of any size.
>
> SR, Vol. 21, No. 4, pp. 786-89.
> R: Paul L. Horecky.

127. KINGSBURY, Robert C. and Robert N. Taafe. An
      Atlas of Soviet Affairs. New York, Praeger, 1965.
      153p. $4.00, cloth; $1.75, paper.

> This handy atlas serves as an introduction
> to many aspects of Soviet life and is a use-
> ful tool for general information. Short
> chapters on over 60 subjects will guide the
> high school student into further and more
> comprehensive study of the Soviet Union.

128. LENSEN, George Alexander. The Soviet Union:
      An Introduction. New York, Appleton-Century-
      Crofts, 1967. 181p. $1.95, paper.

> A handbook-like treatment of the Soviet
> Union, stressing geography, history, eco-
> nomics, government, education, religion
> and art. Numerous photographs exemplify
> Soviet life. The narrow scope of discussion
> of various topics is adaptable to high school
> rather than college use.

129. MAXWELL, Robert. ed. and comp. Information
      U.S.S.R.: An Authoritative Encyclopedia about the
      Union of Soviet Socialist Republics. Oxford,
      Pergamon Press, 1962. 982p. $30.00.

> Compiled in cooperation with the editors of
> the Great Soviet Encyclopedia, the encyclo-
> pedia purports to make available the facts
> about the Soviet Union as seen through the
> eyes of official Soviet institutions. The
> reader in search of objective information
> should keep this fact in mind.

> SR, Vol. 22, No. 1, pp. 186-87.
> R: Sergius Yakobson

130. The Soviet Union: An Introduction to the Geography,
      Peoples, History, and Political Structure of the USSR.
      By the editors of Scholastic Book Services. New
      York, Scholastic Book Services, 1965. 160p. $0.65,
      paper. (Scholastic World Affairs Multi-Text, No. 2)

The book is directed primarily at secondary school students. It is extremely brief and written in a simple, direct style. It provides sketches and basic information as the subtitle explains.

SR, Vol. 24, No. 1, pp. 161-62.
R: John M. Thompson

131.   UTECHIN, Sergej V. Everyman's Concise Encyclopedia of Russia. London, Dent; New York, Dutton, 1961. 623p. $7.95, cloth; $2.65, paper.

This is an up-to-date reference source of distinct usefulness. Some 2050 articles range over Russian matters from Abkan to Zyryans, furnishing information of the kind that the general reader is most likely to ask and that the reference librarian is often hard pressed to find. Students on all levels will use this book to their advantage.

SR, Vol. 21, No. 1, p. 187-88.
R: R. V. Allen

132.   WHITING, Kenneth R. The Soviet Union Today: A Concise Handbook. Rev. edition. New York, Praeger, 1966. 434p. $7.50, cloth; $2.95, paper.

A handbook of general information for any library to support effective teaching and reference services. A well-selected bibliography for suggested in-depth reading increases substantially the value of this comprehensive work.

SR, Vol. 22, No. 2, pp. 349-50.
R: Lawrence Krader

B.   Bibliographies

(See also bibliographies under RUSSIA and EASTERN EUROPE)

133.　CLEMENS, Walter C. Jr. ed. Soviet Disarmament
Policy, 1917-1963: An Annotated Bibliography of
Soviet and Western Sources. Stanford, Calif.,
Hoover Institution on War, Revolution and Peace,
Stanford University, 1965. 151p. $4.00.

134.　HAMMOND, Thomas T. ed. Soviet Foreign Relations
and World Communism: A Selected, Annotated
Bibliography of 7,000 Books in 30 Languages.
Princeton, N.J., Princeton University Press, 1965.
1240p. $25.00.

> A comprehensive reference tool, this volume
> is essential for college libraries for daily
> use by student and teacher. Because of its
> scope, the publication will probably not be
> equalled soon.
>
> SR, Vol. 25, No. 1, pp. 173-74.
> R: Fritz T. Epstein

135.　HORECKY, Paul L. ed. Basic Russian Publications:
An Annotated Bibliography on Russia and the Soviet
Union. Chicago, University of Chicago Press, 1962.
313p. $6.50.

> 1396 entries, the majority of which are in
> Russian language.
>
> SR, Vol. 25, No. 2, p. 370-72.
> R: Fritz T. Epstein

136.　Institute for the Study of the USSR, Institute Publications (1951-1964). Comp. by Max Klieber.
Munich, Institut zur Erforschung der USSR, 1965.
131p. $2.00.

> This bibliography contains a multiple-approach
> index: title, subject, author.

137.　SHAPIRO, David. comp. A Select Bibliography of
Works in English on Russian History, 1801-1917.
Oxford, Basil Blackwell, 1962. 106p. 10s 6d.

Outstanding articles from periodicals are
included in addition to books.

SR, Vol. 25, No. 2, pp. 370-72.
R: Fritz T. Epstein

C. Biographies

138.   COOLIDGE, Olivia. Makers of the Red Revolution.
Boston, Houghton Mifflin, 1963. 240p. $3.75.

A series of seven brief and readable biographies on Marx, Lenin, Trotsky, Stalin, Tito,
Khrushchev, and Mao Tse-Tung designed for
the student and younger reader. In spite of
some errors, this popular treatment well
serves its purpose.

SR, Vol. 24, No. 2, pp. 161-63.
R: John M. Thompson

139.   CRANKSHAW, Edward. Khrushchev: A Career.
New York, Viking, 1966. 320p. $7.50.

This political biography of Khrushchev is
broadly conceived, dramatically presented,
and eminently readable. It abounds in
insights into the phenomenon of Khrushchev.

SR, Vol. 26, No. 3, pp. 492-93.
R: Carl A. Linden

140.   DEUTSCHER, Isaac. Stalin: A Political Biography.
Fair Lawn, New Jersey, Oxford University Press,
1949. 631p. $8.75; 2nd ed., New York, Oxford
University Press, 1967. 661p. $12.50, cloth;
$2.95, paper.

The author, a former Menshevik who knew
Stalin personally has portrayed the late
dictator in a remarkably objective way.
Recommended as reference material for
college libraries.

141. DEUTSCHER, Isaac. Trotsky. Vol. I: The Prophet
Armed. Trotsky, 1879-1921. 540p.; Vol. II: The
Prophet Unarmed. Trotsky, 1921-1929. 508p.;
Vol. III: The Prophet Outcast. Trotsky, 1929-1940.
562p. Fair Lawn, N.J., Oxford University Press,
1954-1963. 3 Vols. $9.50 each.

>A most comprehensive and perceptive biogra-
>phy of Trotsky by one of his followers which
>should be available in college libraries.

142. FISCHER, Louis. The Life of Lenin. New York,
Harper & Row, 1964. 703p. $12.50, cloth; $2.95, paper.

>One of the best Lenin biographies in the
>English language. The author shows Lenin
>to be essentially a political realist who was
>quick to seize the opportunities that presented
>themselves. The work is richly supplied with
>material for reference and supplementary
>reading. As a whole, this scholarly account
>is more for the specialist than the nonspecialist
>who would lack the necessary background in
>history.
>
>SR, Vol. 24, No. 1, pp. 121-22.
>R: Saul N. Silverman

143. PAYNE, Robert. The Life and Death of Lenin.
New York, Simon & Schuster, 1964. 672p. $8.50.

>A well-balanced and unbiased story about
>Lenin. A similar account is contained in:
>David Shub. Lenin: A Biography. Garden
>City, N.Y., Doubleday, 1948. 438p.

144. PAYNE, Robert. The Rise and Fall of Stalin. New
York, Simon & Schuster, 1965. 767p. $10.00.

>A lengthy biography of Stalin. Mr. Payne
>uses a wide range of Russian and foreign
>materials pertaining to the late dictator,
>including documents and memoirs that have
>been published under Khrushchev. The book

reveals much curious information, some of which still awaits proof.

SR, Vol. 25, No. 2, pp. 343-44.
R: Francis B. Randall

145. PISTRAK, Lazar. The Grand Tactician: Krushchev's Rise to Power. New York, Praeger, 1961. 296p. $6.75. (Praeger Publications in Russian History and World Communism, No. 87)

An excellent biography of Khrushchev, one of the closest lieutenants of Stalin. Well documented, this study illuminates all phases of Khrushchev's life and his role in the Soviet power structure.

146. POSSONY, Stefan T. Lenin: The Compulsive Revolutionary. Chicago, Regnery, 1964. 418p. $7.95. (Hoover Institution Publications)

A Lenin biography which is presented from a different point of view. Possony claims that Lenin, always his own master, was willing to destroy the existing order simply for the sake of destruction.

SR, Vol. 24, No. 1, pp. 121-23.
R: Saul N. Silverman

147. RIGBY, T. H. ed. Stalin. Englewood Cliffs, N.J., Prentice-Hall, 1966. 182p. $4.95, cloth; $1.95, paper.

A new approach in the evaluation of Stalin's life and the role he played. The author sees Stalin as the actual creator of Leninism because he proved able to present complex ideas clearly and simply and to grasp what was essentially new and peculiar to Lenin's Marxism. Stalin is introduced, in his own words, as tactician, public orator and ideologist of his own distinctive brand of Communism. Comments by four reputable

scholars on Communism-E. H. Carr,
George Kennan, Robert H. McNeal, and
R. C. Tucker-on Stalin's place in history
increase the value of the book. Advanced
students should take advantage of this publication.

148. RUSH, Myron. The Rise of Khrushchev. Washington, Public Affairs Press, 1958. 116p. $3.25.

This book deals with the question of how
Khrushchev succeeded in ousting his rivals
and becoming the ranking Soviet leader. It
answers the question by showing that he did
so through Stalin's method, namely by using
the office of secretary of the Party as a
jumping board. The book is suggestive as
well as informative.

SR, Vol. 17, No. 3, pp. 359-61.
R: Alfred G. Meyer

149. SCHULZ, Heinrich E. and Stephen S. Taylor. eds.
Who's Who in the USSR 1961/62: A Biographical
Dictionary Containing about 400 Biographies of
Prominent Personalities in the Soviet Union, Com-
piled by the Institute for the Study of the USSR,
Munich, Germany. Munich, New York, Scarecrow
Press, 1962. 964p. $21.00. 2nd ed.: 1966.
1189p. $25.00.

The most detailed and up-dated biography
on prominent Soviet personalities in the
English language.

SR, Vol. 22, No. 4, pp. 786-87.
R: Paul L. Horecky

150. WOLFE, Bertram D. Three Who Made a Revolution:
A Biographical History. New York, Dial Press,
1948. 661p. $5.00; Boston, Beacon Press, 1959.
661p. $2.95, paper.

The author, the former director of TASS,
presents a portrait of Lenin as a man of

unswerving devotion to his cause, of Trotsky
designed to restore Lenin as a man of great
stature, and of Stalin as "the most striking
example in all history of a man who has
succeeded in inventing himself. " The author's
sympathies with Lenin do not reduce the value
of this biographical study.

SR, Vol. 8, No. 3, pp. 227-29.
R: Rohn N. Hazard

151. WOLFENSTEIN, E. Victor. The Revolutionary
Personality: Lenin, Trotsky, Gandhi. Princeton,
Princeton University Press, 1967. 330p. $7.50.

Focusing on the personalities of three well
known revolutionaries, the author elaborates
on the question - what attributes of personality enable an individual to become an effective revolutionary leader, what is responsible
for a gain of power?

D. Communism

(See also special chapter on Communism)

152. The Anti-Stalin Campaign and International Communism:
A Selection of Documents. Edited by Russian Institute,
Columbia University. New York, Columbia University
Press, 1956. 338p. $1.75, paper.

In this much-needed collection, the text of
Nikita Khrushchev's "secret" speech,
delivered on February 25, 1956, at the
Twentieth Congress of the Communist
Party, is followed by shocked, semi-rebel-
lious, or semi-applauding statements by
several Western Communist leaders, and
by editorials form Western Communist
newspapers. The collection furnishes a
vast amount of important material for study
and research.

SR, Vol. 26, No. 3, pp. 397-99.
R: Albert Parry

153. ASPATURIAN, Vernon V. The Soviet Union in the
World Communist System. Stanford, Calif., Hoover
Institution on War, Revolution and Peace, Stanford
University, 1966. 96p. $2.50 (Hoover Institution
Publications, No. 13)

> The imprint of the Soviet Union upon the
> Communist world is ineradicable. This
> study explores the relationship of the USSR
> to the Communist-Party states.

154. DAN, Theodore. The Origins of Bolshevism. Translated by Joel Carmichael. Preface by Leonard
Shapiro. New York, Harper & Row, 1965. 468p.
$10.00.

> The author, a long-time leader of the Men-
> sheviks, analyzes the multiple elements in
> nineteenth- and early twentieth-century
> Russian socialism which constitute the
> background of the Russian Revolution of
> 1917. Rare bibliographical references are
> of distinct value for further reading and
> research. Recommended for advanced
> students of Russian history.

155. DANIELS, Robert V. The Conscience of the Revolution: Communist Opposition in Soviet Russia.
Cambridge, Harvard University Press, 1960.
256p. $10.00. (Russian Research Center Studies,
No. 40)

> This work is a unique contribution to the
> understanding of Soviet Communism because
> it discusses the internal opposition that
> developed in the party at crucial stages in
> its history. Despite the complexity of the
> issues treated, this engaging study will
> make rewarding reading for the student
> with general background in Russian history.

SR, Vol. 21, No. 1, pp. 162-63.
R: Herbert J. Ellison

156. DJILAS, Milovan. Conversations with Stalin.
Translated by Michael B. Petrovich. New York,
Harcourt, Brace & World, 1962. 214p. $3.95,
cloth; $1.65, paper.

> A memoir by the former vice president of
> Yugoslavia describing three visits to Moscow
> and his encounters there with Stalin. This
> account should be recommended as required
> literature for students of Russian affairs.

157. KOLARZ, Walter. Communism and Colonialism:
Essays. Edited by George Gretton. Introduction
by Edward Crankshaw. New York, St. Martin's
Press, 1964. 147p. $4.95.

> The author discusses the impact of the
> Communist tyranny on oppressed and
> captive peoples and nations and also
> stresses the Communist threat to mankind
> in its entirety. Mr. Kolarz devotes
> particualr attention to the status of the
> nations within the Soviet Union proper
> that are being russified as they were in
> the days of Tsarism. This volume is a
> definite asset to a library collection.

> SR, Vol. 24, No. 1, pp. 137-38.
> R: Stefan T. Possony

158. LENIN, V.I. What Is To Be Done? Translated by
S.V. and Patricia Utechin. Edited, with an intro-
duction and notes, by S.V. Utechin. Oxford,
Oxford University, Clarendon Press, 1963. 213p.
$4.00.

> Still regarded in the Soviet Union as a work
> which "laid the foundations of the ideology of
> the Bolshevik Party, " this discourse by
> Lenin is the master key to understanding
> Communist political action today. The

editorial sketches of historical and party
background add to the usefulness of the
publication.

SR, Vol. 23, No. 3, p. 596.
R: Nathan Smith

159.   MEYER, Alfred G. Leninism.   Cambridge, Harvard
University Press, 1957. 324p. $5.50; New York,
Praeger, 1962. $2.50, paper.

The author successfully answers the question:
What is Leninism? The book is thus not a
full treatment of Leninism but a systematic
exposition of Lenin's theory and practice,
justified and limited by their survival value.
The author fully commands Lenin's voluminous
writings and his clear exposition of Lenin's
ideas is enriched by comparisons with Marx
and other Socialist thinkers.

JMH, Vol. 31, No. 4, pp. 394-95.
R: Carl E. Schorske

160.   PAGE, Stanley W.   Lenin and World Revolution.
New York, New York University Press, 1959.
270p. $5.00.

A study in Lenin's concept of Communist
revolution, with particular concentration
on the years 1917-1920. The account
follows Lenin's changing views which
accommodated changing situations within
and outside Soviet Russia. The student of
political science may use this volume for
helpful references.

161.   POSSONY, Stefan T. ed.   Lenin Reader. Chicago,
Regnery, 1966. 528p. $10.00 (Hoover Institution
Publications, No. 15)

Expertly selected, essential writings by
Lenin, topically and chronologically
arranged. Recommended for students of

Soviet affairs as introduction into Leninist philosophy.

162. RIEBER, Alfred J. and Robert C. Nelson. A Study of the USSR and Communism: An Historical Approach. Chicago, Scott-Foresman, 1962. 272p. $1.35, paper; New York, Putnam's, 1964. 256p. $3.95, cloth.

> This volume is especially noteworthy for its attention to questions of cultural and intellectual history and to the cultural ferment which has been so prominent a part of Soviet life since 1953. It offers a very clear picture of the nature and extent of intellectual dissent in the Soviet Union and Eastern Europe during the past decade.
>
> SR, Vol. 23, No. 1, pp. 161-62.
> R: Herbert J. Ellison

163. RIEBER, Alfred J. and Robert C. Nelson. eds. The USSR and Communism: Source Readings and Interpretations. New York, Scott-Foresman, 1964. 320p. $2.95, paper.

> Selected readings on important issues. The material lends itself to high school use and should also be found in college libraries.

164. SCHAPIRO, Leonard. The Origin of the Communist Autocracy. Political Opposition in the Soviet State: First Phase 1917-1922. London, for London School of Economics and Political Science, Bell, 1955, 397p. 35s; Harvard University Press, $8.25; New York, Praeger, 1965. 416p. $2.95, paper.

> This book, better than any other, explains how and why Lenin defeated his rivals and seized power within the Russian Communist Party. Carefully documented analysis of emergence of dictatorship in the Soviet Union. A first-rate contribution to the literature on Russian revolution.

165. SWEARER, Howard R. and Richard P. Longaker. eds. <u>Contemporary Communism</u>: Theory and Practice. Belmont, Calif., Wadsworth, 1963. 405p. $5.25, cloth; $3.95, paper. (Wadsworth Continuing Education Series)

> A competent selection of readings for use by students of high school and college. Excerpts range from the classics of Marxism-Leninism and the 1961 Program of the Communist Party of the Soviet Union to analytical studies by Western specialists to round out a comprehensive picture of the role and appeal of Communist ideology and of major facets of the Soviet system. The selection also includes matters of foreign policy of the Communist countries.
>
> SR, Vol. 24, No. 1, pp. 161-62.
> R: John M. Thompson

166. TOMPKINS, Stuart Ramsey. <u>The Triumph of Bolshevism</u>: Revolution or Reaction? Norman, University of Oklahoma Press, 1967. 331p. $5.95.

> This volume completes the author's trilogy on Russian thought and character. The book examines the heritage of Bolshevism and its features as revealed by their social, ideological, political and economic policies. Bolshevism in action does not perform identically with the aims set up by Marxism.

167. U. S. Congress. House. Committee on Un-American Activities. <u>The Crimes of Khrushchev</u>. Washington, U. S. Govt. Printing Office, 1959. In 7 parts.

> Several reputable specialists were among the consultants.

E. Communist Party

168.   ARMSTRONG, John A.   The Politics of Totalitarianism: The Communist Party of the Soviet Union from
1934 to the Present.   New York,   Random House,
1961.   458p. $7.50.

> The most crucial and decisive years of the
> history of the Communist Party are examined
> in this account by a historian and political
> scientist who has mastered the instruments of
> research.   Yet the unproportionate emphasis
> on power structures tends to neglect the
> importance of personal motives, hence
> Stalin's role is not sufficiently explained.
> Of special merit is a comprehensive bibli-
> ography of sources which will render this
> work more useful in the hands of advanced
> students.
>
> SR, Vol. 21, No. 3, pp. 555-57.
> R: Ronald Thompson

169.   AVTORKHANOV, Abdurakham.   The Communist
Party Apparatus.   Chicago, Regnery, 1966.   422p.
$10.00.   (Foundation for Foreign Affairs)

> Unlike any other book on this topic, this one
> offers first hand experiences.   Its author
> was a member of the Communist Party of
> the Soviet Union from 1927 to 1937.   His
> experiences on different levels and in many
> responsible positions equipped him with an
> insight unmatched by Western scholars.   The
> book is systematically arranged, lucidly
> written and packed with details of functional
> characteristics of the apparatus.   The stu-
> dent of Soviet affairs will find this story most
> revealing.

170.   The Great Purge Trial.   Edited, with Notes by
Robert Tucker and Stephen F. Cohen.   Introduction

by Robert C. Tucker. New York, Grosset &
Dunlap, 1965. 725p. $5.95.

Examination of recently published records
of the March, 1938, trial in the light of all
the relevant information known to the editors,
with particular stress on the purpose of the
trial. The Great Purge is remembered as
a most dramatic period in the history of the
Communist Party thus making this volume
indispensable for students of Soviet affairs.

SR, Vol. 25, No. 2, pp. 353-55.
R: Robert M. Slusser

171. GRULIOW, Leo. ed. Current Soviet Policies:
Vol. I: The Documentary Record of the 19th Communist Party Congress and the Reorganization
After Stalin's Death. New York, Praeger, 1953.
268p. $5.00. Vol. II: A Documentary Record of
the Twentieth Communist Party Congress and Its
Aftermath. New York, Praeger, 1957. 250p.
$6.50.

Selected translations of the Current Digest
of the Soviet Press.

SR, Vol. 13, No. 1, pp. 117-20.
R: G. Theodore Mitau

172. LAQUEUR, Walter Z. and Leopold Labedz. eds.
The Future of Communist Society. New York,
Praeger, 1962. 196p. $5.00.

A collection of articles analyzing the CPSU
Program of 1961. Useful for the advanced
student.

173. The New Society: Final Text of the Program of the
Communist Party of the Soviet Union. With Annota-
tions and an Introduction by Herbert Ritvo. New
York, The New Leader, 1962. 251p. $0.75, paper.

Text of the program of the CPSU adopted
by the Twenty-second Party Congress in 1961.

174. RESHETAR, John S. Jr. <u>A Concise History of the Communist Party of the Soviet Union.</u> Rev. Ed. New York, Praeger, 1964. 381p. $7.00, cloth; $2.50, paper.

> This work is built on the theme that Lenin provided the presumptions that culminated in Stalin's great purge. Lenin was as ruthless, obsessed, headstrong, self-righteous, and confident as his successor, not the kindly humanitarian driven to severity by circumstances, as he is sometimes pictured. Stalin's difference lay in his creation of the apparatus of oppression, the organization. For beginners, the volume is probably too condensed to be meaningful; advanced students will need to rely on it.

> AHR, Vol. 66, No. 1, pp. 162-64.
> R: John N. Hazard

175. SCHAPIRO, Leonard. <u>The Communist Party of the Soviet Union.</u> New York, Random House, 1964. 631p. $7.50, cloth; $2.65, paper. Vintage Books.

> The author, a well known authority on Soviet affairs, offers in this work the most comprehensive history of the Communist party in Russia ever written in English. The personal experiences he gained while living in Russia and the critical method he employed in his analysis have produced a history the interested reader has long been waiting for. Based on a thorough command of elusive sources, this book offers an authoritative, comprehensive and lively account of the origins, evolution and thinking of the Soviet party leadership. Getting familiar with this publication should be in the interest of any responsible citizen and inquiring young student.

176. SCHAPIRO, Leonard. ed. <u>The U. S. S. R.</u> and the
     <u>Future</u>: An Analysis of the New Program of the
     CPSU. New York-London, Praeger (for the
     Institute for the Study of the USSR, Munich), 1963.
     324p. $6.00, cloth; $2.50, paper.

     > Collection of essays on the new Party pro-
     > gram (1961). The text of the 1919 and 1961
     > party programs is appended. Recommended
     > for classroom use.

177. TRISKA, Jan F. ed. <u>Soviet Communism</u>: Program
     and Rules; Official Texts of 1919, 1952 (1956), and
     1961. San Francisco, Chandler, 1962. 196p. $1.50,
     paper.

     > This volume offers an accurate translation
     > of the 1961 party program of the CPSU with
     > comments on all changes made since 1919.
     > Useful for students of Soviet affairs. A
     > necessary title for college library reference
     > services.

178. WOLFE, Bertram D. ed. <u>Khrushchev and Stalin's</u>
     <u>Ghost</u>: Text, Background and Meaning of Khrush-
     chev's Secret Report to the Twentieth Congress on
     the Night of February 24, 1956. New York, Praeger,
     1957. 322p. $3.95.

     > The author attempts to analyze what he calls
     > "the most important document ever to have
     > come from the Communist movement" and
     > "the most damning indictment of the Soviet
     > system ever to have been made be a Soviet
     > leader." This book should be made requir-
     > ed reading on all levels of teaching.

     > JMH, Vol. 29, No. 3, pp. 303-4.
     > R: H. Gordon Skilling

F.   Education

179.   DE WITT, Nicholas. Soviet Professional Manpower: Its Education, Training and Supply. Washington, D. C., National Science Foundation, 1955. 257p. $1.25.

> Statistical data regarding vocational training and employment.

180.   DE WITT, Nicholas. Education and Professional Employment in the U.S.S.R. Washington, D. C., National Science Foundation, 1961. 856p. $5.50.

> This standard work on Soviet education is still the most comprehensive and scholarly study in the English language. But it embraces much more, giving an account in great detail, of the entire program for the training of specialists of all occupational levels, from skilled worker to research scientist. The systems of the military and party schools are examined. Superb primary sources were used to document this study, going far beyond any other report on Soviet education. A classic study highly recommended for all types of libraries.
>
> SR, Vol. 21, No. 3, pp. 568-69.
> R: George S. Counts

181.   GOROKHOFF, Boris I. Publishing in the U.S.S.R. Bloomington, Indiana University Publications, 1959. 306p. $3.00. (Slavic and East European Series, Vol. 29)

> All aspects of book printing are treated in this book. An impressive general survey of the publishing activities and their ramifications in the USSR. The profusion of supplementary charts, tables, and lists makes this study an invaluable source of information.
>
> SEEJ, Vol. 7, No. 4, pp. 432-33.
> R: Viktor Koeressar

182.   GRANT, Nigel. Soviet Education. Baltimore,
        Penguin Books, 1964. 190p. $0.95, paper.

> Helpful account of the general features of
> the Soviet school system, up-dated to about
> 1963, and overall reliable in its content and
> observations. A brief treatment of the sys-
> tem for the general reader; the specialist
> will have to rely on De Witt's work.

> SR, Vol. 24, No. 3, pp. 574-75.
> R: George Z. F. Bereday

182a.   JOHNSON, Priscilla. Khrushchev and the Arts:
        The Politics of Soviet Culture. Cambridge, Mass.,
        M.I.T. Press, 1965. 300p. $7.50.

> This work portrays a regime that is first, on
> the warpath against a too-rapid increase of
> intellectual ferment and finally, in retreat
> when confronted by the steadfastness of the
> writers and artists themselves. It offers
> a glimpse of the link between cultural policy
> and other dilemmas facing the Soviet
> Communist Party.

182b.   KOROL, Alexander G. Soviet Research and Develop-
        ment: Its Organization, Personnel, and Funds.
        Cambridge, Mass., M.I.T. Press, 1965. 375p.
        $11.00.

> This volume surveys the background and
> development of the recent changes in the
> organizational structure of the Soviet
> research and development establishment
> and analyzes Soviet published data on the
> scale and the rate of growth of the research,
> the number of institutions, the size and
> composition of the scientific labor force
> involved, and the research and budget.

183.   MEDLIN, William K., Clarence B. Lindquist, and
        Marshall L. Schnitt. Soviet Education Programs.

Washington, U. S. Govt. Printing Office, 1960.
281p. $1.25.

> Instruction programs and teacher education
> for primary and secondary schools are dis-
> cussed.

> SR, Vol. 20, No. 3, pp. 550-51.
> R: Nicholas De Witt

184. ROSEN, Seymour M. Higher Education in the USSR:
Curriculum, Schools and Statistics. Washington,
U. S. Office of Education, 1963. 195p. $1.00.

> Extensive, but non-analytical compilation
> of basic information translated from Soviet
> sources. Statistical data on students,
> faculty, institutions, enrollments is provided.
> For information on supervision and quantita-
> tive aspects of Soviet education, see the same
> author's "Higher Education in the USSR,"
> in Dimensions on Soviet Economic Power,
> Washington, Joint Economic Committee of
> the U. S. Congress, 1962. pp. 269-304.

G. Economy and Economic Conditions

185. BERNSTEIN, Morris and Daniel R. Fusfeld. eds.
The Soviet Economy: A Book of Readings. Homewood, Ill. , Irwin, 1962. 382p. $4.50.

> Among available readers on the Soviet
> economy, this one is best suited for high
> school and junior college use. A list of
> carefully selected articles provides supple-
> mentary reading adaptable to courses of
> principles of economics and comparative
> economic systems.

> SR, Vol. 23, No. 2, p. 375.
> R: Benjamin Ward

185a. BRODERSEN, Arvid. <u>The Soviet Worker</u>: Labor and Government in Soviet Society. New York, Random House, 1966. 278p. $4.95, cloth; $1.95, paper.

> The author offers a critical chronological survey of Soviet labor policies from 1917 to the present. Problems of ideology, economic policy, industrial development, education, and social mobility are analyzed.
>
> SR, Vol. 26, No. 4, pp. 688-89.
> R: Peter J. Potichnyj

185b. BROWN, Emily Clark. <u>The Soviet Trade Unions and Labor Relations</u>. Cambridge, Harvard University Press, 1966. 394p. $6.95.

> A large part of this study is devoted to trade union organization and activity at the national, regional, local, and plant levels, but the book also deals with some aspects of Soviet labor policy and industrial relations.
>
> SR, Vol. 26, No. 4, pp. 688-89.
> R: Peter J. Potichnyj

186. CAMPBELL, Robert W. <u>Soviet Economic Power</u>: Its Organization, Growth, and Challenge. Boston, Houghton Mifflin, 1960. 209p. $1.95; 2nd ed., 1966. 184p. $2.75, paper.

> The author's lucid and readable treatment offers an excellent survey of Soviet economy. This study is highly recommended for high schools and colleges, even as a textbook. The general reader will find it most profitable, too.
>
> SR, Vol. 20, No. 2, pp. 331-32.
> R: John P. Hardt

187. HOLZMAN, Franklyn D. ed. <u>Readings on the Soviet Economy</u>. Chicago, Rand McNally, 1962. 763p. $5.95.

A well balanced collection of over forty
articles and excerpts from books dealing
with major aspects of the Soviet economy.
Useful in connection with any textbook on the
Soviet economy. Another recently published
volume of readings: Shaffer, Harry G. The
Soviet Economy. New York, Appleton-Century-
Crofts, 1963. 456p. $4.25.

188.   JASNY, Naum. Soviet Industrialization, 1928-1952.
Chicago, University of Chicago Press, 1961. 467p.
$10.00.

A comprehensive and systematic review of
developments during Stalin's years in power.
Major sectors of the economy such as
industry, agriculture, retail trade, and
consumption are dealt with. While the
book was written by a specialist for students
of Soviet affairs, it can be utilized by begin-
ners because it offers basic information of
the function of the economy under a totalitarian regime.

SR, Vol. 22, No. 2, pp. 356-58.
R: Donald R. Hodgman

189.   LAIRD, Roy D. Collective Farming in Russia:
A Political Study of the Soviet Kolkhozy. Lawrence,
University of Kansas Publications, 1958. 176p.
$2.50.

The author examines both the internal structure of the collective farm as a political
microcosm and the network of political
institutions which tie it to the central
government and make it an organic part
of the Soviet political macrocosm. The
book follows a historical approach: it
takes a broad look at the growth of agricul-
tural socialism from the nineteenth-century
mir to the most recent liquidation of the
MTS.

SR, Vol. 18, No. 4, pp. 608-9
R: Alexander Vucinich

190. MAZOUR, Anatole G. <u>Soviet Economic Development.</u>
Princeton, N.J., Van Nostrand, 1967. 192p. $1.45.

> Russia's economic development from 1917 to
> the Khrushchev-Kosygin policy of co-existence
> is narrated in objective terms. The book can
> be recommended for survey courses.

191. NOVE, Alec. <u>The Soviet Economy</u>: An Introduction.
New York, Praeger, 1961. 328p. Rev. ed.: 1965.
380p. $7.00, cloth; $2.50, paper.

> Mr. Nove's book still remains a landmark
> and standard work for the study of Soviet
> economy. Undergraduates will appreciate
> the clarity of the text and the scope of
> material that it discusses. It also serves
> as an excellent reference tool.

191a. SCHWARTZ, Harry. <u>Russia's Soviet Economy.</u>
2nd ed. New York, Prentice-Hall, 1954. 682p.

> As the first successful textbook on the sub-
> ject for college use, this comprehensive
> work on the Soviet economic system is now
> somewhat dated, nevertheless, it is most
> useful as an introductory text.

192. SCHWARTZ, Harry. <u>The Soviet Economy Since
Stalin.</u> Philadelphia, Lippincott, 1965. 256p.
$5.00.

> As a calm and well-written study, touching
> selectively on the main weaknesses and
> strengths of Communist economies, this
> book should prove profitable to a wide
> audience of non-specialists. Teachers
> will find the account helpful for class
> assignments and scholars in other fields
> of Slavic affairs may use it as valuable
> guide to recent Soviet economic history.

SR, Vol. 25, No. 4, pp. 708-9.
R: Holland Hunter

193. SPULBER, Nicholas. The Soviet Economy: Structure, Principles, Problems. New York, Norton, 1962. 311p. $5.95.

> The book "examines the basic assumptions and the working principles of the Soviet economy as viewed by Soviet economists themselves" and contrasts Soviet with Western concepts. It serves as a handy summary of the intricacies of Soviet national income accounting, choice of alternative investments, and a myriad of other Marxist measures. Though not clearly written, the book is a useful reference with a large amount of material not available elsewhere.

> SR, Vol. 22, No. 1, pp. 167-68.
> R: Judith Thornton

194. SPULBER, Nicholas. Soviet Strategy for Economic Growth. Bloomington, Indiana University Press, 1964. 175p. $4.50.

> This volume offers both the specialist and the lay reader a succinct analysis of the economic debates of the 1920's. It examines alternative goals and strategies of economic development, concepts of economic growth and efficiency, and planning theory and practice.

> SEEJ, Vol. 9, No. 2, p. 232.
> R: Morris Bornstein

195. SWIANIEWICZ, S. Forced Labor and Economic Development: An Enquiry into the Experience of Soviet Industrialization. London-New York, Oxford University Press, 1965. 321p. $9.00.

> This work is the result of personal experience and subsequent research. The author spent

three years (1939-1942) in the Soviet Union
in various capacities. The book offers an
analysis of economic background and an
investigation of economic and social conditions within the forced labor camps. Recommended for the reader interested in economic development and in the function of a
totalitarian regime.

CSS, Vol. 1, No. 1, pp. 143-44.
R: Janis Labsvirs

196. ZALESKI, Eugene. Planning Reforms in the Soviet
Union, 1961-1966: An Analysis of Recent Trends
in Economic Organization and Management. Transl.
by Marie-Christine MacAndrew and G. Warren
Nutter. Chapel Hill, University of North Carolina
Press, 1967. 203p. $6.00.

This volume presents a number of less
known ideas, facts and details pertaining
to current and prospective economic reforms in the USSR.

H. Espionage

197. DALLIN, David J. Soviet Espionage. New Haven,
Yale University Press, 1955. 558p. $5.75.

This is still the most complete and detailed
account of Soviet espionage told in a single
publication. It centers on the Soviet spy
network in Europe and the Western hemis-
phere. The reader will be introduced to
the importance of Soviet espionage, its
working system and the dangers the free
world is still facing. The general public
as well as the student will benefit from this
account.

SR, Vol. 16, No. 3, pp. 423-25.
R: Harry N. Howard

198. HUTTON, J. Bernard. School for Spies: The ABC of How Russia's Secret Service Operates. New York, Coward-McCann, 1962. 222p. $3.95.

> Hutton's book is particularly useful in enlightening people who believe that Communism is on its way out. It reads like a science fiction mystery, and, if even part of it is true, the reader will be disturbed and alerted, for we have nothing to compare with the Russian spy system; it cannot exist in a democracy.

> SR, Vol. 22, No. 2, pp. 351-53.
> R: Kurt L. London

I. Foreign relations — General

199. ADAMS, Arthur E. ed. Readings in Soviet Foreign Policy: Theory and Practice. Boston, Heath, 1961. 420p. $3.85.

> A reasonable mixture of Soviet documents and speeches with narrative and analytical excerpts or articles by non-Soviet authors. The Soviet material consists largely of pronouncements by Lenin and Stalin. Selection of Western authors is rather one-sided. To guide and interpret the dialectic of Marxist thought, the teacher will need a good background in Russian history when using this reader.

> SR, Vol. 21, No. 2, pp. 366-67.
> R: John C. Campbell

200. BELOFF, Max. Foreign Policy of Soviet Russia, 1929-1936; Vol. 2: 1936-1941. London-New York, Oxford University Press, 1947-49. 2 Vols. $4.50, $6.00, respectively. (Issued under the auspices of the Royal Institute of International Affairs)

An excellent record of Soviet diplomatic
actions which followed the Locarno Pact.
The analytical approach adds to the understanding of some Soviet moves.

SR, Vol. 7, No. 1, pp. 95-97.
R: Philip E. Mosely

SR, Vol. 9, No. 2, pp. 131-33.
R: C. Dale Fuller

201. BISHOP, Donald G. ed. Soviet Foreign Relations:
Documents and Readings. Syracuse, N. Y., Syracuse University Press, 1952. 223p. $3.75, paper.

Selection of translated documents on various
aspects of Soviet foreign policy. Though
efficient organization is lacking, undergraduates and even high school students can
profit from these translated documents.

202. BOUSCAREN, Anthony T. Soviet Foreign Policy:
A Pattern of Persistence. New York, Fordham
University Press, 1962. 187p. $5.00.

An overall treatment of Soviet foreign relations. The presentation, in the form of an
anthology, stresses some fundamentally
important concepts of Soviet foreign policy.
The author does not see any notable changes
in Soviet objectives.

AHR, Vol. 68, No. 2, pp. 451-53.
R: John A. Armstrong

203. BRINKLEY, George A. The Volunteer Army and
Allied Intervention in South Russia, 1917-1921:
A Study in the Politics and Diplomacy of the Rus-
sian Civil War. Notre Dame, Ind., University of
Notre Dame Press, 1966. 446p. $8.95.

The author discusses the problem of the
crusade against Bolshevism as it affected
Western diplomacy. He emphasizes the
conflicting views among the statesmen and

military leaders. Mr. Brinkley concludes
that intervention failed not because of the
Red Army or Lenin's tactics but because
aid from the West was inadequate.

204. DALLIN, Alexander. ed. <u>Soviet Conduct in World</u>
<u>Affairs:</u> A Selection of Readings. New York,
Columbia University Press, 1960. 318p. $4.50.

Perspective, challenging, and skillfully
written articles on Soviet foreign relations
were selected for this reader. This well-
balanced material lends itself to be used by
undergraduates and in class discussions.

SR, Vol. 20, No. 1, pp. 134-35.
R: Alvin Z. Rubinstein

205. DALLIN, David J. <u>Soviet Foreign Policy After</u>
<u>Stalin.</u> Philadelphia, Lippincott, 1961. 543p.
$7.95.

Thoroughly documented general survey of
Soviet foreign policy since Stalin's death.
The author demonstrates intimate knowledge
of the Soviet system, thus his explanation
of methods and aims appear to be more
reliable than similar accounts on this topic.
Recommended for advanced students of
Soviet history and foreign affairs.

206. DEGRAS, Jane T. comp. <u>Calendar of Soviet Docu-</u>
<u>ments on Foreign Policy, 1917-1941.</u> London-New
York, Royal Institute of International Affairs, 1948.
248p. $8.00.

Arranged chronologically and by countries,
this collection lists a great number of Soviet
treaties and agreements together with important documents, speeches, interviews and
newspaper articles.

207. DEGRAS, Jane T. ed. <u>Soviet Documents on Foreign</u>
<u>Policy.</u> Vol. I: 1917-1923; Vol. II: 1925-1932;

Vol. III: 1933-1941. London-New York, Oxford University Press, for the Royal Institute of International Affairs, 1951-1953. 3 Vols. $8.00 each volume.

>An excellent collection of diplomatic documents on Soviet foreign policy which constitutes an indispensable source for the student of Soviet policy.

208. EUDIN, Xenia J. and Robert C. North. Soviet Russia and the East, 1920-1927: A Documentary Survey. Stanford. Stanford University Press, 1957. 482p. $10.00. (Hoover Institution Publications, No. 25)

209. EUDIN, Xenia J. and Harold H. Fisher. Soviet Russia and the West, 1920-1927: A Documentary Survey. Stanford. Stanford University Press, 1957. 514p. $10.00. (Hoover Institution Publications, No. 26)

>These two volumes represent a significant addition to the documents available in English on the early period of Soviet foreign policy. No less valuable is the analytical history of this formative period provided in each volume. Nearly all the documents (most of them contained in the Hoover Library) are translations of published material, the greater part of which was previously available only in Russian. The value of these volumes as sources is greatly enhanced by comprehensive analytical bibliographies. These features make the two publications a most important aid to scholarly pursuit as well as a comprehensive introduction for students.

>JMH, Vol. 30, No. 1, pp. 70-71.
>R: John A. Armstrong

210.   EUDIN, Xenia J. and Robert M. Slusser. eds.
Soviet Foreign Policy, 1928-1934: Documents and
Materials. Vol. I. University Park, Pennsylvania
State University Press, 1966. 353p. $9.50.

> The authors selected and translated the
> most important documents and provided
> a brief narrative summary of the main de-
> velopments of the period.

211.   FISCHER, Louis. The Soviets in World Affairs:
A History of Relations Between the Soviet Union
and the Rest of the World. 1917-1929. London-
New York, Cape & Smith, 1930. 2 Vols. $15.00;
New York, Vintage Books, 1960. 616p. $1.85,
paper.

> This classic study of the international rela-
> tions of the Soviet Union, from the Treaty
> of Brest-Litovsk down to the resumption of
> diplomatic relations with Great Britain in
> 1929, represents a thorough work of investi-
> gation and documentation. The author's
> personal acquaintance with leading Soviet
> personalities of that time lends even greater
> value to his interpretation. This study has
> a definite place in the library and in the
> classroom.

212.   GOLDMAN, Marshall I. Soviet Foreign Aid. New
York, Praeger, 1967. 265p. $8.50.

> A thoroughly documented study of Soviet
> foreign aid. The historical account also
> treats the satellite aid programs in con-
> junction with Soviet efforts. The informed
> layman and the specialized student will
> profit from reading this study of an important
> field.

213.   GOODMAN, Elliot R. The Soviet Design for a
World State. With a Foreword by Philip E.
Mosely. New York, Columbia University Press,

1960. 512p. $6.75. (Studies of the Russian Institute, Columbia University)

> The author argues that the Soviet government is, and always has been, dedicated to the long-range goal of a world-wide socialist state in which the Russians will play the dominant role. He demonstrates his point partly by generous quotations from the writings of Communist leaders, and partly by surveying the record of Soviet history since 1917.

> AHR, Vol. 68, No. 1, pp. 136-37.
> R: Richard Pipes

214. KENNAN, George F. Russia and the West Under Lenin and Stalin. Boston, Little-Brown, 1961. 411p. $5.75; New York, Mentor, 1962. 384p. $0.95, paper.

> A series of lectures of Ambassador Kennan are presented in a charming form of communication with the reader. The author's experiences and scholarship place considerable value on his views and interpretations. Though personal political motivations are here exposed to a point of debate, the keen insight into Soviet behavior is challenging to both scholar and layman.

> AHR, Vol. 67, No. 1, pp. 87-88.
> R: Herbert Feis

215. KENNAN, George F. Soviet Foreign Policy, 1917-1941. Princeton, N.J., Van Nostrand, 1960. 184p. $1.45, paper. (Anvil Originals)

> A brief survey of Soviet foreign policy which is interpreted with a personal point of view of the former ambassador to the USSR. Recommended for advanced students as topic for discussion, although unsuitable as textbook.

> SEER, Vol. 39, No. 93, pp. 555-56.
> R: P. A. Reynolds

216. LEDERER, Ivo J. ed. <u>Russian Foreign Policy</u>:
Essays in Historical Perspective. New Haven,
Yale University Press, 1962. 620p. $12.50, cloth;
$2.95, paper.

> This collection of essays is an excellent
> scholarly effort and a major contribution to
> the understanding and teaching of Russian
> history and foreign relations. The publica-
> tion resulted from a symposium held at Yale
> University in 1961, for the purpose of exami-
> ning Russian foreign relations over the past
> century and giving special consideration to
> the elements of continuity and change in
> major aspects of that subject. The book
> contains eighteen articles. No other single
> volume throws so much light on Russian
> foreign relations, providing rich material
> for discussion and study.

> SR, Vol. 22, No. 1, pp. 149-50.
> R: Alan D. Ferguson

217. LIBRACH, Jan. <u>The Rise of the Soviet Empire</u>.
A Study of Soviet Foreign Policy. New York,
Praeger, 1964. 382p. $7.50, cloth; $2.50,
paper. Rev. ed. 1965. 407p. $2.95, paper.

> The book relates the complex story of Soviet
> expansion over the last forty-odd years. It
> is comprehensive, informative and interesting.
> It provides the general reader with a good
> synthesis of Soviet foreign policy, and it
> underscores for the specialist the basic
> assumptions underlying this policy. This
> volume is deserving of a place in the
> college library and classroom.

> JMH, Vol. 37, No. 2, p. 284.
> R: Piotr S. Wandycz

218. McKENZIE, Kermit E. <u>Comintern and World
Revolution, 1928-1943</u>: The Shaping of Doctrine.
New York, Columbia University Press, 1964.
368p. $6.50.

The book contains Comintern statements, resolutions, programs, speeches, and pronouncements from 1928 to 1963, with an appropriate introduction covering the prior nine years. This documentary history of the Comintern adds useful material to the study of Soviet foreign policy.

AHR, Vol. 70, No. 3, pp. 783-84.
R: Theodore H. Von Laue

219. MacKINTOSH, J. M. Strategy and Tactics of Soviet Foreign Policy. London, New York, Oxford University Press, 1962. 332p. $8.00.

A detailed inspection of Moscow's policies abroad since 1944. In nineteen carefully constructed and balanced chapters the book traces the unfolding of Soviet strategies in Europe, Asia and Africa. Soviet-American confrontation continues to be the "main front" of Soviet foreign policies. It is an objective survey of post-war Soviet policies.

SR, Vol. 22, No. 2, pp. 348-49.
R: Charles B. McLane

220. MOSELY, Philip E. The Kremlin and World Politics: Studies in Soviet Policy and Action. New York, Random House, 1960. 557p. $1.65, paper; Vintage Books.

The author, an eminent student of Soviet affairs, presents in this volume a selection of articles which he wrote in the past quarter-century to aid in the understanding of the "Russian problem." The effort illustrates the American viewpoint over an extended period of time offering the student of Soviet foreign policies challenging and interesting reading.

221. MOSELY, Philip E. ed. The Soviet Union, 1922-1962: A Foreign Affairs Reader. Foreword by Hamilton Fish Armstrong. New York-London, Praeger,

published for the Council on Foreign Relations,
1963. 495p. $6.95, cloth; $2.25, paper.

> This book, a selection of thirty articles,
> contains an abundance of interesting material
> which appeared over a forty-year period and
> has almost documentary value. A particularl
> attractive feature of the collection is the
> variety of viewpoints: noted Western scholars
> appear side by side with Soviet authorities.

> SR, Vol. 23, No. 3, pp. 498-99.
> R: George von Rauch

222. OLIVA, L. Jay. ed. Russia and the West: From
Peter to Khrushchev. Boston, Heath, 1965. 289p.
$6.50, cloth; $2.50, paper. (D.C. Heath Studies
in History and Politics)

> (See entry No. 77)

223. RUBINSTEIN, Alvin Z. ed. The Foreign Policy of
the Soviet Union. New York, Random House, 1960.
457p. $6.50; 2nd ed. 1966. 458p. $4.95, paper.

> The purpose of this work is to increase "the
> student's understanding of the nature of the
> contemporary Soviet challenge." Useful
> to elementary study, the book is less suited
> for advanced students.

> SR, Vol. 20, No. 1, pp. 125-27.
> R: Jan F. Triska

224. SHAPIRO, Leonard. ed. Soviet Treaty Series:
A Collection of Bilateral Agreements and Conven-
tions, etc., Concluded Between the Soviet Union
and Foreign Powers. Washington, Georgetown
University Press, 1950-55. Vol. I: 1917-1928,
237p.; Vol. II: 1929-1939. 425p. $10.00 and
$12.00, respectively.

> Excerpts of significant treaties, the collection
> is of unsurpassed value for the study of inter-
> national affairs of the Soviet Union.

225. SHULMAN, Marshall D. Stalin's Foreign Policy Reappraised. Cambridge, Harvard University Press, 1963. 320p. $6.50. (Russian Research Center Studies, No. 48)

> This volume deals with changes in Soviet foreign policy during the last years of Stalin's dictatorship, showing clearly that Stalin's death did not mark a sharp break in continuity. Though strictly limited in its temporal scope, this book can furnish insights into the present situation and even permit reasonable anticipation of the future.

> JMH, Vol. 38, No. 1 pp. 116-17.
> R: Jesse D. Clarkson

226. SLUSSER, Robert M. and Jan F. Triska. A Calendar of Soviet Treaties 1917-57. Stanford. Stanford University Press, and London. Oxford University Press, 1959. 530p. $15.00. (Hoover Institution Publications)

> Invaluable source for all students of Soviet affairs, this book consists of an elaborate calendar, not only of the treaties entered into by the Soviet regime, but of all other traceable international agreements to which the Soviet Union has been a party. References to the full text of treaties are given.

> SEER, Vol. 39, No. 93, p. 571.
> R: Max Beloff

227. SNELL, John L. ed. The Meaning of Yalta: Big Three Diplomacy and the New Balance of Power, Baton Rouge, Louisiana State University Press, 1956. 239p. $3.75.

> Several contributors present the American view on the agreements of Yalta of 1945. They conclude that the unhappy results were due rather to the bad faith of the Kremlin than to the folly of Churchill or Roosevelt.

This controversial publication can stimulate class room discussion on the subject.

JMH, Vol. 39, No. 2, pp. 165-66.
R: Dexter Perkins

228. THOMPSON, John M. Russia, Bolshevism, and the Versailles Peace. Princeton, Princeton Unversity Press, 1966. 429p. $11.50. (Studies of the Russian Institute, Columbia University)

The Russian problem at the Paris Peace Conference consisted of three elements: boundaries, diplomatic claims, and minority problems; then the question of power in Russia, and finally Bolshevism. The author examines motives which guided the participants while dealing with these obstacles. The work offers a full account of one of the major diplomatic problems of the twentieth century.

CSS, Vol. 1, No. 2, pp. 327-28.
R: Eugene P. Trani

228a. TRISKA, Jan F. and David D. Finley. Soviet Foreign Policy. New York, Macmillan, 1968. 544p. $9.95.

The work provides an explanation and analysis of Soviet foreign policy and the factors influencing her behavior in the international system. Soviet policy is examined within the International Communist system, in the developing countries of Asia, Latin America, Africa and the capitalist countries.

229. WARTH, Robert D. The Allies and the Russian Revolution: From the Fall of the Monarchy to the Peace of Brest-Litovsk. Durham, N.C., Duke University Press, 1954. 294p. $4.50.

A highly readable account of the official and unofficial relations between democratic and Bolshevik Russia and the other major

Allied Powers during the first year of the revolution. This book is a welcome addition to the literature on World War I and the Russian Revolution. A very helpful annotated bibliography is appended.

JMH, Vol. 28, No. 3, pp. 290-91.
R: Robert Paul Browder

230. WARTH, Robert D. Soviet Russia in World Politics. New York, Twayne, 1963. 544p. $7.50.

This work fills a gap in the literature on Soviet affairs with a running chronological narrative of Soviet Russia's foreign relations from the Revolution to 1962. The book is well suited for quick reference or as an introduction to the subject.

AHR, Vol. 69, No. 2, pp. 461-62.
R: Robert V. Daniels

J. Foreign Relations — with individual countries

231. BISHOP, Donald Gordon. The Roosevelt-Litvinov Agreements: The American View. Syracuse, N.Y., Syracuse University Press, 1965. 297p. $7.50.

The establishment of diplomatic relations between the United States and the Soviet Union in November 1933 was accompanied by the signing of a series of agreements. The author takes up each of the agreements and surveys the record of its implementation by the Soviet Union. It is a valuable contribution not only to modern history and diplomacy but also to statecraft.

JMH, Vol. 39, No. 2, p. 207.
R: Robert M. Slusser

232. BRANDT, Conrad. Stalin's Failure in China, 1924-
1927. Cambridge, Harvard University Press, 1958.
226p. $4.75. (Russian Research Center Studies,
No. 31)

Dramatic history of Stalin's policy in China.
Myth, illusion, ecclesiastical pietism: these
brought on Russia's fiasco in China. This is
a book that ought to be read by everyone
seriously interested in an incongruous but
important chapter in modern history.

SR, Vol. 19, No. 2, pp. 303-4.
R: Nathaniel Peffer

233. BROWDER, Robert Paul. The Origins of Soviet-
American Diplomacy. Princeton, Princeton University Press, 1953. 256p. $6.00, cloth; $2.95,
paper.

A useful treatment of the history of Soviet-
American relations. The author has made
available considerable factual material.

SR, Vol. 13, No. 3, pp. 442-43.
R: Frederick C. Barghoorn

234. CARR, Edward Hallet. German-Soviet Relations
Between the Two World Wars, 1919-1939. New York,
Harper & Row, c. 1951, 1966. 146p. $1.25, paper.

The British historian presents his view on
German-Soviet relations in a lucid and
altogether excellent survey. The lay reader
and junior college student will be especially
rewarded by this narrative.

235. DALLIN, Alexander. The Soviet Union at the United
Nations: An Inquiry into Soviet Motives and Objectives. New York, Praeger, 1962. 256p. $6.00,
cloth; $1.95, paper. (Praeger Publications in
Russian History and World Communism, No. 106)

This is one of the important studies in
English on the subject. The author is

exceptionally well qualified to examine the
Soviet conduct in the UN and his account can
be regarded as standard treatment. The
book concentrates on timely problems and
offers a comprehensive analysis and sound
judgment.

AHR, Vol. 68, No. 2, p. 451-52.
R: John A. Armstrong

236. DYCK, Harvey L. Weimar Germany and Soviet
Russia, 1926-1933. New York, Columbia University
Press, 1966. 279p. $6.75.

Enlightening discussion of German-Soviet
cooperation during the Weimar Republic
period, especially between the Reichswehr
and the Red Army.

237. FARNSWORTH, Beatrice. William C. Bullitt and
the Soviet Union. Bloomington, Indiana University
Press, 1967. 244p. $7.50.

This revealing portrait of W. C. Bullitt's
career in the United States diplomatic
service between 1914 and 1945 focuses on
his role in the peace program of Woodrow
Wilson and his influence on Soviet-American
relations during the Roosevelt administration.

238. FISCHER, Louis. Russia, America and the World.
New York, Harper, 1961. 245p. $4.50.

A critical evaluation of Soviet domestic and
foreign policy against the background of
Russian national interest. Interesting and,
at various points, controversial conclusions
about the nature of the Soviet state under
Stalin, providing a wealth of material for
constructive class discussions.

239. FLOYD, David. Mao Against Khrushchev: A
Short History of the Sino-Soviet Conflict. New

York-London, Praeger, 1964. 456p. $7.50, cloth; $2.95, paper.

> This account narrates the Sino-Soviet split as it developed between 1956 and 1963, supported by an extensive chronology of documents and significant events. Well researched and readable, this is a valuable compendium for the general reader and student of Communist affairs.

> SR, Vol. 23, No. 3, pp. 597-98.
> R: Kurt L. London

240. FREUND, Gerald. Unholy Alliance. New York, Harcourt, Brace, 1957. 283p. $6.00.

> This study provides the fullest account to date of German-Russian relations in the period from the Treaty of Brest-Litovsk to the Treaty of Berlin (1918-1926). The author throws new light on certain aspects of these relations. Students of international affairs should not overlook this title. A valuable addition to the growing literature on this subject.

> JMH, Vol. 30, No. 4, pp. 378-79.
> R: Zygmunt J. Gasiorowski

241. GRIFFITH, William E. Sino-Soviet Relations, 1964-1965. Cambridge, Mass., M.I.T. Press, 1967. 425p. $7.50.

> A chronological continuation of the author's The Sino-Soviet Rift, treating the period from November, 1963, through November, 1965. Detailed analytical assessment of several aspects of Sino-Soviet relations for that particular period.

242. GRIFFITH, William E. The Sino-Soviet Rift. Cambridge, Mass., M.I.T. Press, 1964. 512p. $7.95, cloth; $2.95, paper.

The author considers the Sino-Soviet rift as
the single most significant ideological split
since the Reformation in the sixteenth century. A chronological summary, analysis
and documentation of the developments in
the Sino-Soviet dispute between February,
1962 and November, 1963 is contained in
this treatment.

243. KAPUR, Harish. Soviet Russia and Asia 1917-1927:
A Study of Soviet Policy towards Turkey, Iran and
Afghanistan. New York, Humanities Press, 1967.
266p. $8.50.

A penetrating study of Soviet foreign policy
in the first decade of Soviet power in regard
to Russia's immediate neighbors in Asia.
This book also sheds light on Leninism and
Lenin's understanding of the importance of
nationalism in Asia.

244. KENNAN, George F. Soviet-American Relations,
1917-1920. Vol. I: Russia Leaves the War;
Vol. II: The Decision to Intervene. Princeton,
Princeton University Press, 1956-1958. 2 Vols.
$10.00 each.

Ambassador Kennan discusses events from
November, 1917 to March, 1918 in the first
volume; in the second he carries the study
down to the American landing in North
Russia and Siberia. A detailed, authorita-
tive and expertly composed account of
Soviet-American relations from which
advanced students can gain information and
insight.

245. KOCHAN, Lionel E. Russia And the Weimar
Republic. Cambridge, England, Bowes and Bowes,
1954; New York, Praeger, 1955. 190p. $4.25.

The book deals with diplomatic and military
relations as well as with the relations between

the Communist International and the Communist Party of Germany (KPD). An excellent bibliography is also furnished.

246. MEHNERT, Klaus. Peking and Moscow. Translated from German by Lelia Vennewitz. New York, Putnam's, 1963. 522p. $6.95.

A comparison of the two countries and cultures as well as their relationship in recent years. The author's extensive personal experience in both countries qualifies him to speak with authority on this problem.

247. ROBERTS, Henry L. Russia and America. New York, Harper, 1956. 251p. $3.50.

The theme of the book is the question, what policy should the United States pursue regarding Communist totalitarianism in the nuclear age. The author has no doubt that even in this age America must, if necessary, be prepared to accept general war to prevent the world-wide establishment of Communism. This stimulating and expert presentation of a timely topic is well suited for classroom use.

SR, Vol. 16, No. 1, pp. 82-83.
R: George Bolsover

248. ROSENBAUM, Kurt. Community of Fate: German-Soviet Diplomatic Relations, 1922–1928. Syracuse, N.Y., Syracuse University Press, 1965. 325p. $6.75.

This book is in large part a biography of Count Ulrich Brockdorff-Rantzau, a German Ambassador to the Soviet Union, who favored a Russo-German alliance. In addition Germany's military cooperation with Russia, including manufacture of poison gas in the Soviet Union, is examined in this piece of painstaking research. The study is an excellent and praiseworthy account of Russo-

German relations in the 1920's.

JMH, Vol. 38, No. 1, pp. 115-16.
R: M. C. Wren

249. RUBINSTEIN, Alvin Z. The Soviets in International Organizations: Changing Policy toward Developing Countries, 1953-1963. Princeton, Princeton University Press, 1964. 380p. $7.50.

> The Soviet policy toward developing countries can be studied in the context of the United Nations. The aim underlying the Soviet Union's participation in this international body is to exploit it for political propaganda. The author describes with considerable skill such Soviet activity in the various UN economic agencies. The reader gets a clear message from this sober account: the operation of the Soviet government is not predictable and cannot be measured by conventional methods used by Western countries.

> SEER, Vol. 44, No. 2, pp. 255-56.
> R: Harry Hanak

250. SCOTT, William E. Alliance Against Hitler: The Origins of the Franco-Soviet Pact. Durham, N.C., Duke University Press, 1962. 296p. $7.50.

> This excellent volume treats the labyrinth of European politics in the early 1930's. The author concentrates on the internal and external pressures on France which culminated in the signing of the pact on May 2, 1935.

251. TARULIS, Albert N. Soviet Policy Toward the Baltic States, 1918-1940. Notre Dame, Ind., University of Notre Dame Press, 1959. 276p. $5.50.

> The book centers on the events of 1918-19 and 1939-40. The author's main objective

is examination of the theory and practice of
Soviet national and diplomatic policy, and in
so doing he points up very sharply the double
standard that permeates the Soviet attitude.
This study is a rare contribution to a neglected area of American scholarship.

SR, Vol. 19, No. 4, pp. 597-99.
R: Alfred Erich Senn

252. Territorial Claims in the Sino-Soviet Conflict: Documents and Analysis. Hoover Institution on War,
Revolution and Peace. Stanford. Stanford University Press, 1965. 77p. $2.50.

A study of the border question in the Sino-
Soviet conflict, based on official statements,
press releases and monitored broadcasts
from Russian, Chinese and Japanese sources.

253. WILLIAMS, William A. American-Russian Relations
1781-1947. New York, Rinehart, 1952. 367p.
$5.00.

(See entry No. 79)

254. ULLMAN, Richard H. Anglo-Soviet Relations, 1917-
1921. Vol. I: Intervention and the War. Princeton,
Princeton University Press, 1961. 360 p. $7.50.
Vol. II: The Search for Accord--in preparation.

This first exhaustive study in English on
Anglo-Soviet relations, projected for a
two-volume publication, covers the period
from the Bolshevik Revolution to the
Compiégne Armistice in November, 1918.
The author elaborates with marked success
on British policy which in sum was too
pragmatic to deal effectively with the chaotic
situation in Soviet Russia. Since official
British records are still not available to
historians, the study cannot claim to be
complete, nevertheless, it is clearly and

effectively written and represents a very desirable contribution to the period under discussion.

SR, Vol. 21, No. 2, pp. 351-352.
R: Victor S. Mamatey

255. WEINBERG, Gerhard L. Germany and the Soviet Union, 1939-1941. Leiden, Netherlands, Brill, 1954. 210p. 19 Guilders. (Studies in East European History)

A useful treatment of the episode of Nazi-Soviet relations reconstructed in a concrete, unbiased report of this crucial period. Students of international affairs will appreciate Weinberg's effort which clarifies some of the decisions that were made in Berlin.

JMH, Vol. 28, No. 3, pp. 295-97.
R: Walter L. Dorn

256. WHEELER-BENNET, John W. Brest-Litovsk: The Forgotten Peace, March 1918. London, Macmillan, 1938; New York, St. Martin's Press, 1966. 478p. $8.00, cloth; $4.95, paper.

The best known and still most valuable treatment of the first Soviet-German Treaty which helped Lenin sustain the Soviet seizure of power in Russia in 1917. First published in Great Britain in 1938, the book stands as one of the classics for that particular period and should be in college library collections.

JMH, Vol. 29, No. 4, p. 429.
R: Dwight E. Lee

257. ZAGORIA, Donald S. The Sino-Soviet Conflict, 1956-1961. Princeton, Princeton University Press, 1962. 484p. $8.50.

The author has assembled an overwhelming number of facts and documents intended to convince the reader that specific traits in the development of Russian and Chinese Communism and differences in tactics are irrefutable indications that the conflict between the two countries is expanding and international Communism is disintegrating.

SR, Vol. 21, No. 4, pp. 756-57.
R: Richard Wraga

K. Coexistence

258. BERZINS, Alfred. The Two Faces of Coexistence. New York, Speller, 1967. 335p. $6.00.

This book is particularly timely in view of recent developments in Communist-dominated parts of the world and the political maneuvers accompanying them. Lenin's therory of capitalist decadence has, according to the author, not yet been abandoned by his heirs.

EE, Vol. 16, No. 7, pp. 59-60.
R: Pavel Korbel

259. GEHLEN, Michael P. The Politics of Coexistence: Soviet Methods and Motives. Bloomington, Ind., London, Indiana University Press, 1967. 334p. $6.75. (Indiana University International Studies)

A comprehensive analysis of the evolution of Russia's policy of coexistence in its ideological, military, economic and political aspects. The author concludes that Soviet ideology is subordinated to Russian national interests.

260. KOVNER, Milton. The Challenge of Coexistence. Washington, Public Affairs Press, 1961, 130p. $3.25.

The author feels that the Soviet Union plans to implement "peaceful coexistence" through

an aggressive economic policy, particularly
in the underdeveloped areas. The benefits
of this policy will be employed by the Soviets
in their economic penetration of underdeveloped countries.

261. KULSKI, Wladyslaw W. Peaceful Coexistence: An
Analysis of Soviet Foreign Policy. Chicago,
Regnery, 1959. 661p. $12.50.

This is an attempt to analyze Soviet foreign
policy in light of available documents. The
author concentrates on two motives of Soviet
foreign policy: the mission to communize
the world, and the desire to preserve the
Soviet state through Russian national interests as the center of world revolution. This
one-man, one-volume effort has produced
the most extensive digest of Soviet statements on foreign affairs thus far available
in English. The author's presentation re-
quires of the reader some background knowledge on the subject.

JMH, Vol. 32, No. 4, pp. 416-17.
R: William B. Ballis

262. RAMUNDO, Bernard A. Peaceful Coexistence:
International Law in the Building of Communism.
Baltimore, Johns Hopkins Press, 1967. 262p.
$6.95.

The author examines the manner in which
the Soviets utilize international law to support policy objectives and compares the
Soviet approach to international law with
that of other countries.

L. Geography

263. COLE, John P. and F.C. German. A Geography of
the U.S.S.R. Washington, Butterworth, 1961. 290p.
$8.95.

Still the most balanced of numerous recent texts for teacher reference. Up-to-date survey of branches of the economy and of economic planning regions at the beginning of the Seven-Year Plan (1959-65) with tables, bibliography and index.

264. CRESSEY, George B. Soviet Potentials: A Geographic Appraisal. Syracuse, N. Y. Syracuse University Press, 1962. 232p. $5.75.

A brief readable survey of the natural conditions, resources, peoples, economy and regions of the Soviet Union. The author attempts to take a critical look at a vast territory which claims to have potential for becoming the world's richest state. Generously interspersed with illustrations and maps, this lively book is rewarding to even the general reader.

SR, Vol. 21, No. 4, p. 764.
R: Chauncy D. Harris

265. FULLARD, Harold. ed. Soviet Union in Maps. London, Philip, 1961. 32p. $1.00.

Colored maps and text. An inexpensive paperbound atlas covering historical, physical, economic, and regional geography. Suitable for general use by the student.

266. HOOSON, David J. M. A New Soviet Heartland? Princeton, N. J., Van Nostrand, 1964. 132p. $1.45, paper.

This study focuses on the Baikal-Volga region and gives a general overview of the USSR. Illustrated maps increase its usefulness. The author describes the factors that make this area of vital importance to the Soviet Union.

267.   HOOSON, David J. M. The Soviet Union: People
and Regions. Belmont, Cal., Wadsworth, 1966.
376p. $7.95.

> A notable attempt to understand the relation-
> ship between population and geographic fac-
> tors. The first part of the volume is topi-
> cally organized containing chapters on the
> natural habitat, historical background, farm-
> ing, industry, transport and distribution of
> population. The second part includes a de-
> scriptive and analytical discussion of the
> regions. Despite some typographical errors
> and a few faulty statistics the book can be
> recommended for students of geography.
>
> SR, Vol. 26, No. 2, pp. 331-34.
> R: Robert A. Lewis

268.   JACKSON, W. A. Douglas. The Russo-Chinese
Borderlands: Zone of Peaceful Contact or Potential
Conflict? New York, London, Van Nostrand, 1962.
126p. $1.45.

> A geographical and historical study of the
> 4,500 miles of the Sino-Soviet frontier,
> including maps, tables, bibliography and
> index.

269.   JACKSON, W. A. Douglas. Soviet Union: A Study
in Depth. Grand Rapids, Mich., Fideler, 1963.
192p. $4.08.

> A well-written and illustrated text for use
> in junior high schools.

270.   LYDOLPH, Paul E. Geography of the U. S. S. R.
New York, Wiley, 1964. 451p. $10.95.

> This is a combination of a general regional
> geography and a systematic economic geog-
> raphy of the country as a whole, making it
> a versatile textbook on Soviet geography.
> Many excellent maps and illustrations add
> to its attractiveness. Recommended for
> undergraduates.

SR, Vol. 23, No. 3, pp. 599-600.
R: W. A. D. Jackson

271. MELLOR, R. E. H. Geography of the U. S. S. R.
London, Macmillan; New York, St. Martin's Press,
1964. 403p. $12.00.

> This volume treats physical features, his-
> torical development, population distribution,
> settlement forms and administrative structure,
> agriculture, fuels and minerals, industry and
> transport for the Soviet Union as a whole in a
> topical approach. It is likely to become popu-
> lar as a quick introduction to that large and
> complex land for the general public.

> SR, Vol. 25, No. 2, pp. 365-66.
> R: George Kish

272. RODIONOFF, Nicholas R. ed. Soviet Geography:
A Bibliography. Two Parts. Washington, Library
of Congress, Reference Department, 1951. 668p.
$2.25.

273. SHABAD, Theodore. Geography of the U. S. S. R. :
A Regional Survey. New York, Columbia University Press, 1951. 584p. $12.00.

> Detailed survey of the Soviet Union by regions
> and oblasts. Valuable reference tool as it
> includes numerous maps, tables, bibliography
> and an extensive index. Though dated, the
> book is recommended for college teaching.

> SR, Vol. 10, No. 4, pp. 320-24.
> R: J. A. Morrison

274. TAAFFE, Robert and Robert Kingsbury. An Atlas
of Soviet Affairs. New York, Praeger, 1965. 150p.
$1.75.

> Small in format but rich on maps with useful
> commentary. Brief introductions and con-
> cise surveys treat various aspects of Soviet
> history, geography, economy, population, etc.

This study is an indispensable addition to any textbook on Soviet geography.

M. History

(For general history see also chapter on Russia — History)

275.   ADAMS, Arthur E. ed. The Russian Revolution and Bolshevik Victory: Why and How. Boston, Heath, 1965. 108p. $1.50. (Problems in European Civilization)

> The list of contributors to this "pro and con" volume includes Russian and Western authors. Its purpose is to stimulate discussions in classrooms and to gain a better understanding of this important event by being challenged with diverse views.

276.   BLACK, Cyril E. ed. Rewriting Russian History: Soviet Interpretation of Russia's Past. New York, Praeger, 1956. 413p. $7.50; Vintage Books, 1962. $1.95, paper. (Praeger Publications in Russian History and World Communism, No. 39)

> Twelve essays discuss the main trends in Soviet historical writing. In light of the meager literature in English on Russian historiography, this study is a welcome addition, particularly for the advanced student.

> SR, Vol. 17, No. 2, pp. 234-35.
> R: Raymond H. Fisher

277.   BUNYAN, James and H. H. Fisher. eds. The Bolshevik Revolution, 1917-1918. Stanford, Stanford University Press, 1961. 735p. $10.00.

> This collection of documents, decrees, manifestos, press reports and other materials tells how the Bolsheviks seized

power in Russia and how they kept it during
the first six months of their rule. The
editorial notes accompanying the documents
summarize the events dealt with.

278.	CARR, Edward Hallet. A History of Soviet Russia.
Vols. 1-3: The Bolshevik Revolution, 1917-1923;
Vol. 4: The Interregnum, 1923-1924; Vols. 5-7:
(3 vols. in 4) Socialism in One Country, 1924-1926.
London, New York, Macmillan, 1950-1964. 7 Vols.
Vols. 1-4 $6.00 each, cloth; Vols. 5 and 6 $7.50
each, Vol. 7 $17.50. Baltimore, Penguin Books,
1966. Vols. 1 and 2 $2.25; Vol. 3 $2.45, paper.

This monumental study contains an incom-
parable wealth of information which should
be used by instructors and must be available
in libraries, though it cannot be recommended
to the beginning student.

279.	CARSON, George Barr, Jr. Russia Since 1917.
Washington, D.C., AHA Service Center for
Teachers of History, 1962. 25p. $0.50.

A brief evaluation of the most important
titles dealing with the Soviet period of
Russia's history. Chronological reviews
serve as helpful guides to the history of
the USSR.

280.	CHAMBERLIN, William Henry. The Russian
Revolution 1917-1921. Vol. I: From the Overthrow
of the Czar to the Assumption of Power by the
Bolsheviks, 1917-1918; Vol. II: From the Civil
War to the Consolidation of Power, 1918-1921.
New York, Grosset and Dunlap, 1965. 2 Vols.
$2.65 each, paper.

A revised edition of a work which was published in 1948 and still maintains a leading
place among studies dealing with the Soviet
revolution. A chronological record of
events between 1917 and 1921. An advanced
student of Soviet affairs will find the book
indispensable.

281.   DALLIN, David J. From Purge to Coexistence: Essays on Stalin's and Khrushchev's Russia. Chicago, Regnery, 1964. 289p. $6.95. (Foundation for Foreign Affairs Series, No. 8)

> The collection of essays exhibits scholarship, insight, and sober analysis of the subject. These essays were written between 1957 and 1960 by a well-known scholar of Soviet affairs. The book should be regarded as indispensable for college education.

> AHR, Vol. 71, No. 3, pp. 1024-25.
> R: Oliver H. Radkey

281a. FILENE, Peter G. Americans and the Soviet Experiment 1917-1933. Cambridge, Harvard University Press, 1967. 389p. $7.95.

> Recorded reactions of American business, American labor, and of a cross-section of American intellectuals to the Russian revolution and the Soviet regime in the period when it was not officially recognized by Washington.

282.   FOOTMAN, David. Civil War in Russia. New York, Praeger, 1962. 328p. $8.00.

> A good survey of the subject. The story is told in a series of episodes or aspects of the war; each related to the role of one of the centers of the struggle. The author expresses his ideas clearly. He also writes with objectivity and insight, treating persons and events on their own merits. The book is significant for the general as well as the more specialized reader.

> SR, Vol. 22, No. 4, pp. 760-61.
> R: John Albert White

282a. LAQUEUR, Walter. The Fate of the Revolution: Interpretations of Soviet History. New York, Macmillan, 1967. 216p. $5.95.

283. LYONS, Eugene. Worker's Paradise Lost: Fifty Years of Soviet Communism: A Balance Sheet. New York, Funk & Wagnalls, 1967. 350p. $6.95.

> For fifty years, Russia has been the stage of a vast human tragedy. In this book the Soviet drama is told act by act: the Bolshevik seizure of power, the planned society, the purges and persecutions, the famines and Siberian camps, the rise of a new aristocracy. The author indicates that the de-Stalinization program and the so-called liberal policies of the current regime are Communist myths.

284. MAMATEY, Victor S. Soviet Russian Imperialism. Princeton, N.J., Van Nostrand, 1964. 192p. $1.45, paper. (Anvil Originals, No. 68)

> This rare study describes in historic terms the evolution of Soviet imperialism. The author contends that Soviet imperialism is an empirically observable and pragmatically provable fact. This book merits to be included in reading list for any student of Soviet affairs.

285. PAGE, Stanley W. ed. Russia in Revolution: Selected Readings in Russian Domestic History Since 1855. Princeton, N. J., Van Nostrand, 1965. 299p. $3.75, paper.

> The editor presents in these selections a living picture of what the people of Russia experienced and suffered in the period of great changes. Five major sections present views of contemporaries, latter-day historians, and other writers. Many readings are translated here for the first time.

286. PIPES, Richard. The Formation of the Soviet Union: Communism and Nationalism, 1917-1923. Cambridge, Harvard University Press, 1954. 286p.

$6.50. Rev. ed. 1964. 365p. $7.95. (Russian Research Center Studies, No. 13)

> Excellent, among the outstanding contribu-
> tions to an understanding of nationalism and
> its development as a political phenomenon
> in the non-Russian areas of the old tsarist
> empire. The book deals with the Soviet
> conquest of the Ukraine, Belorussia, and
> the Moslem territories. Lenin's exploitation
> of national sentiments of the non-Russians has
> received a commendable scholarly treatment.
> The study is important for library and class-
> room use.

> JMH, Vol. 29, No. 1, pp. 153-54.
> R: George Barr Carson, Jr.

287. RANDALL, Francis B. Stalin's Russia: An Historical Reconsideration. New York, Free Press, 1965;
London, Collier-Macmillan. 328p. $6.95.

> This lively essay is intended to show that
> the key to understanding Stalin's Russia
> lies in Stalin himself rather than in some
> of the impersonal historical forces pointed
> to by other analysts. The book's consider-
> able value is as a text supplement in under-
> graduate courses in Russian history. Senior
> high school students can readily use this clear
> narrative.

> SR, Vol. 25, No. 3, pp. 699-700.
> R: Sidney Heitman

288. REED, John. Ten Days that Shook the World. Fore-
word by V. I. Lenin; Introd. by Granville Hicks.
New York, Modern Library, 1935. 371p. $0.95;
New York, Random House, Vintage Books, 1965.
$1.45, paper.

> The American journalist John Reed, who
> later became a Communist, managed to get
> to Russia in time to witness the October

Revolution. In this book he gives a detailed day-by-day account of events as they took place during that fateful period. It is an illuminating historical document which has become essential literature of the Bolshevik revolution.

289. SALISBURY, Harrison E. Moscow Journal: The End of Stalin. Chicago, University of Chicago Press, 1961. 450p. $6.95.

The New York Times correspondent in the Soviet Union from March, 1949 to October, 1953, provides a day-by-day account of a crucial period in Russia's history. He concludes that recent changes in the Soviet foreign policy are not primarily due to changes in the leadership. This book also contains examples of distorted stories by the New York Times about Soviet life due to the Soviet censorship and the editors' managing of news reporting.

SR, Vol. 22, No. 2, pp. 345-46.
R: John A. Armstrong

290. TREADGOLD, Donald W. ed. The Development of the USSR: An Exchange of Views. Seattle, University of Washington Press, 1964. 416p. $6.50, cloth; $2.95, paper.

Nine discussions by twenty-eight contributors which were originally published in the Slavic Review are available in this book. The arrangement is by subjects: Soviet Union, Old Russia, Russia's Western Borderlands, Russia Between East and West. The reader, whatever his specialty, will profit from the wide range of contributions in history, political science, economics, and literature. A most worthwhile publication in its category.

SEEJ, Vol. 9, No. 3, pp. 349-50.
R: Thomas Riha

291. VON LAUE, Theodore H. Why Lenin? Why Stalin?
A Reappraisal of the Russian Revolution, 1900-1930.
Philadelphia, Lippincott, 1964. 242p. $3.95, cloth;
$1.95, paper.

> The book is designed both as a brief summary
> of the turbulent years between the political
> revolution of 1905 and Stalin's economic
> revolution of the 1920's, and as a general
> interpretation of the position of Soviet
> Russia in modern history. Useful and
> critical, stimulating and provocative, the
> study is well suited for class discussion and
> as supplementary reading.

SR, Vol. 23, No. 4, pp. 748-50.
R: Cyril E. Black

N. History — Textbooks

(For more texts see also chapter: Russia)

292. DMYTRYSHYN, Basil. The U.S.S.R.: A Concise
History. New York, Scribner, 1965. 620p.
$5.00, paper.

> A well written one-volume history of the
> USSR. Chronological organization and a
> broad survey-style treatment make this
> title acceptable as a textbook for under-
> graduate studies. A 300-page appendix
> contains important documents, such as
> Khrushchev's de-Stalinization speech of
> 1956 and the Programme of the CPSU of
> October 31, 1961.

293. RAUCH, Georg von. A History of Soviet Russia.
Translated from the German by Peter and Annette
Jacobsohn. New York, Praeger, 1957. 493p.

5th Rev. ed. 1967. 554p. $8.50, cloth; $2.50, paper.

A brief treatment, one of the best, of Soviet Russian history. Though not critical enough in its extensive elaboration of domestic developments, it compensates with excellence on chapters of Soviet foreign policy. Its use as a textbook is limited to more advanced students yet it serves well as a handy reference for instructors.

JMH, Vol. 30, No. 1, pp. 69-70.
R: Leopold H. Haimson

294. TREADGOLD, Donald W. Twentieth Century Russia. Chicago, Rand McNally, 1959. 550p. $7.00. 2nd ed. 1964. 576p. $8.50.

A superior textbook on the modern period of Russia's history. Well organized, easily read, with an annotated bibliography, the volume contains helpful tables on population, party congresses, Politburo members, heads of state and indices of economic production.

SR, Vol. 21, No. 3, pp. 542-44.
R: Oliver H. Radkey

O. Historiography

295. PUNDEFF, Marin. ed. and comp. History in the U.S.S.R.: Selected Readings. San Francisco, Cal., Chandler, 1967. 313p. $6.50. (Hoover Institution Publications)

The only available collection of readings on Soviet historiography in English. Brief essays by Marx, Engels, Plekhanov, Lenin, Stalin, Pokrovsky, Khrushchev, A. M. Pankratova, N. L. Rubinshtein, in addition to numerous documents, decrees and statements which offer an insight into Soviet

historiography, interpretation and changes.
An excellent bibliography increases the
value of this publication for instructional
use.

296. SHTEPPA, Konstantin F. Russian Historians and
the Soviet State. New Brunswick, N.J., Rutgers
University Press, 1962. 437p. $10.00.

This valuable study tells of Soviet historians
and historiography whose services have been
subordinated to the Communist ideology. The
author's first-hand experiences, until 1941,
lend more weight to the account. Soviet
historiography underwent several revisions
which are discussed at length. This translation from Russian was prepared by William
L. Blackwell and serves as a vital source of
information on the subject.

SR, Vol. 21, No. 4, pp. 744-45.
R: Sergei Pushkarev

P. Law

297. GRZYBOWSKI, Kazimierz. Soviet Legal Institutions:
Doctrines and Social Functions. Ann Arbor, University of Michigan Press, 1962. 285p. $7.50.

The book analyzes the meaning of "socialist
legality," surveys the field of Soviet law
and compares Soviet and Western legal
philosophy.

SEEJ, Vol. 7, No. 2, pp. 226-27.
R: Darrell P. Hammer

298. LAFAVE, W. R. ed. Law in the Soviet Society.
Urbana, University of Illinois Press, 1965. 297p.
$4.75.

A collection of essays on Soviet law. The
book will be read with great interest not

only by lawyers, but also by all students of
Soviet affairs.

SEER, Vol. 45, No. 104, p. 261.
R: Ivo Lapenna

Q. Nationalities

(See also under:
Baltic States (Estonia, Latvia, Lithuania)
Belorussia
Transcaucasian Republics (Georgia, Armenia,
       Azerbaidzhan)
Ukraine
Asian Soviet Republics (Kazakh, Kirghiz,
       Taddjik, Turkmen, Uzbek)

299. CONQUEST, Robert. The Soviet Deportation of
Nationalities. London, Macmillan, 1960. 203p.
New York, St. Martin's Press, $6.75.

An account of the little-known tragic fate of
non-Russian peoples. The author reveals
in a lucid narrative facts pertaining to the
deportation of Volga Germans, Kalmyks,
Crimean Tatars and other smaller ethnic
groups. A historical background is recommended to help understand these events.

299a. CONQUEST, Robert. ed. Soviet Nationalities Policy
in Practice. New York, Praeger, 1967. 160p. $5.2

Based almost entirely on Soviet sources,
this survey traces Soviet nationalities policy
from Lenin's 1903 Party program to the present. Included are such topics as the role of
the Communist Party, the integration of the
nationalities into the Soviet state, the treatment of national culture of individual nationalities, and the opposition and resentment toward the Soviet Russification policies.

300. GURIAN, Waldemar. ed. <u>Soviet Imperialism</u>: Its
      Origins and Tactics. Notre Dame, Ind., Univers-
      ity of Notre Dame Press, 1953. 166p. $2.50.

    Several contributors discuss the develop-
ment of the problem of non-Russian nations
of the USSR. There is a similarity in the
treatment of nationalities by the Tsarist
and Soviet regimes. This informative
volume serves well as an introduction into
one of the most sensitive areas of Russian
affairs.

301. KOLARZ, Walter. <u>Russia and Her Colonies</u>. Lon-
      don, Philip, 1952. 340p. New York, Praeger,
      $6.00. 3rd ed. 1955. $6.00.

    An excellent study of Soviet policy toward
non-Russian nations under Lenin and Stalin.
It is pointed out that the policy of Soviet
colonialism is apparent not only in territorial
expansion but Russification has played an
important role under Tsarist as well as
under Soviet regimes.

302. KRADER, Lawrence. <u>Peoples of Central Asia.</u>
      Bloomington, Indiana University Publications;
      The Haugue, Netherlands, Mouton, 1963. 319p.
      $4.00. (Uralic and Altaic Series, Vol. 26)

    A handbook of Soviet Central Asia and
Kazakhstan containing information on
economy and ecology, languages, history,
religion, family and society, demography
and cities. The book includes maps, an
extensive bibliography, an index and numerous statistical tables.

    SR, Vol. 23, No. 2, pp. 391-94.
    R: Robert A. Rupen

303. LOW, Alfred D. <u>Lenin On the Question of Nationality</u>.
      New York, Bookman Associates, 1958. 103p.
      $4.00.

An important contribution to the problem of the relationship of communism and nationalism. Lenin was the first to exploit national issues for the aims of communism. The study reveals the inconsistencies in Lenin's writings and the distortion of that problem not only under Stalin but even during Lenin's lifetime.

AHR, Vol. 64, No. 1, p. 182.
R: Hans Kohn

304. PARK, Alexander G. <u>Bolshevism in Turkestan.</u> New York, Columbia University Press, 1957. 427p. $6.75.

The study consists of ten chapters on such subjects as the initial steps toward unification of the disintegrating elements within Turkestan, a comparative analysis of Bolshevism and Islam, economic and agrarian policies, land reforms, cultural effects and the general pattern of Soviet nationality policy. The author abstains from drawing any conclusions on his findings. A most welcome addition to historical literature serving advanced students of Soviet affairs.

JMH, Vol. 29, No. 4, pp. 404-5.
R: Anatole G. Mazour

305. SCHLESINGER, Rudolf. ed. <u>Changing Attitudes in Soviet Russia.</u> Vol. 2: The Nationalties Problem and Soviet Administration; Selected Readings on the Development of Soviet National Policy. Translated from the Russian by W. W. Gottlieb. London, Routledge & Paul, 1956. 299p. New York, Humanities Press, 1956. $6.00.

Useful material helping to clarify the question of nationality politics in the Soviet Union and the nature of the federation of the Soviet republics.

306. SETON-WATSON, Hugh. The New Imperialism:
A Background Book. Chester Springs, Pa., Dufour
Editions, c. 1961. 136p. $2.95.

>The author treats the nationality problem
>of nineteenth-century Russia, the Bolshevik
>response to Lenin's program on self-deter-
>mination and subsequent implementation of
>a policy under the Soviet regime similar to
>Tsarist efforts at Russification. The second
>half of this book deals with Moscow's policy
>toward the satellites and new Afro-Asian
>states.

>SEEJ, Vol. 7, No. 4, pp. 439-40.
>R: Norton T. Dodge

307. SMAL-STOCKI, Roman. Captive Nations: Nationalism of the Non-Russian Nations in the Soviet Union.
New York, Bookman Associates, 1960. 118p.
$3.50.

>A case in defense of non-Russian peoples of
>the USSR as seen by a Ukrainian author.
>This writing offers factual explanation of
>nationalist issues in Eastern Europe.

>SR, Vol. 20, No. 1, p. 127.
>R: Michael Rywkin

308. SPECTOR, Ivar. The Soviet Union and the Muslim
World, 1917-1956. Seattle, Distributed by the
University of Washington Press, 1956. 155p.
$3.50.

>The account is well documented and offers
>a survey of events in the Middle East as
>they pertain to the Soviet Union. The main
>topic of this work, however, centers on the
>study of the course of Soviet policy with
>reference to the surrounding Muslim coun-
>tries. The book fills a very urgent need
>in respect to an area that has hitherto
>attracted little attention and is very meagerly

represented in the literature.

SR, Vol. 16, No. 4, pp. 568-70.
R: M. Z. K.

309.   WHEELER, Geoffrey. Racial Problems in Soviet Muslim Asia. 2nd ed. London, Oxford University Press, 1962. 67p. $1.20. (Institute of Race Relations)

> This brief study contains an unbiased picture of the Soviet Central Asian problems. It offers a sound introduction for anyone interested in this particular area of Soviet studies.
>
> SR, Vol. 20, No. 1, pp. 127-28.
> R: Michael Rywkin

310.   ZENKOVSKY, Serge A. Pan-Turkism and Islam in Russia. Cambridge, Harvard University Press, 1960. 345p. $8.00 (Russian Research Center Studies, No. 36)

> Turkic peoples constitute about ten per cent of the total Soviet population. They form in at least four Soviet republics a majority and substantial minorities in several others. Sympathetic presentation in defense of Russia's Moslems.
>
> SR, Vol. 20, No. 1, pp. 137-39.
> R: Firyz Kezemzadeh

R.   Politics and Government

311.   ANDERSON, Thornton. Russian Political Thought: An Introduction. Ithaca, N. Y. Cornell University Press, 1967. 432p. $9.75.

> In this lucid, fully documented history, the author stresses the continuity as well as the evolution of political philosophy and

practice in Russia by examining Russian attitudes toward autocracy, isolationism, and dogma as they developed through the centuries. Marxism-Leninism was a natural development of ideas and attitudes already prevalent among Russian intellectuals. The author sees the present Soviet regime not as a twentieth-century phenomenon but as a powerful, more comprehensive development of traditional political assumptions.

312. ARMSTRONG, John A. Ideology, Politics and Government in the Soviet Union. New York, Praeger, 1962. 160p. Rev. ed. 1967. $5.50, cloth; $1.95, paper.

In this short, but altogether admirable work, the author has undertaken to provide an introduction to the main features of the Soviet political system. It is designed to meet the needs of students who come fresh to the subject and who, for the most part, are unlikely to go beyond it.

SR, Vol. 22, No. 3, pp. 565-66.
R: Merle Fainsod

313. BARGHOORN, Frederick C. Politics in the USSR: A Country Study. Boston, Little-Brown, 1966. 418p. $2.95, paper.

The author attempts to show the Soviet state in its relations with Soviet society. This is a concise and easy-to-read book containing essential information on the real Communist politics. Recommended for study of political science and related fields.

314. BARGHOORN, Frederick C. Soviet Russian Nationalism. New York, Oxford University Press, 1956. 274p. $7.50.

The author shows an exceptionally intense
form of Russian nationalism as the central
element of Soviet ideology. This new brand
is an often bewildering combination of traditional Great Russian nationalism, elements
of Western Marxism, and a system of ration-
alizations of the political order which has
taken shape in the Soviet Union. Russification of non-Russian nationalities is practiced
as in the old days of Tsarist Russia. This
book, better than any other on the subject,
illustrates the peculiarities of Soviet Russian national sentiment.

JMH, Vol. 28, No. 4, p. 406.
R: Joseph S. Roucek

315.   BAUER, Raymond A. et al. eds. How the Soviet
System Works. Cambridge, Harvard University
Press, 1956. 274p. (Russian Research Center
Studies, No. 24) New York, Vintage Press, 1960.
312p. $1. 65, paper.

This study, as part of the Harvard project
on the Soviet social system, is based on
reports and experiences of political refugees, scholars and specialists, which
assure its particular value for the study
of the Soviet world.

316.   BRZEZINSKI, Zbigniew K. Ideology and Power in
Soviet Politics. New York, Praeger, 1962. 180p.
Rev. ed. 1967. 297p. $6. 50, cloth; $2. 50, paper.

An essential interpretive guide for the de-
batable ground of Soviet ideology and practice. The revised edition includes four new
essays in which the author pinpoints the
developing strains in the Soviet political
system, compares the Sino-Soviet doctrinal conflicts with those faced by the Papacy
several centuries ago, assesses the Sino-
Soviet split in terms of its implications for
the West, and analyzes the Russian attitude
toward European integration.

317. CARSON, George Barr, Jr. <u>Electoral Practices in the U.S.S.R.</u> New York, Praeger, 1955. 153p. $3.50. (Praeger Publications in Russian History and World Communism, No. 38)

> The author describes and analyzes the procedures for the conduct of elections in the USSR during two main phases of development, before and after the Constitution of 1936. The election statute of 1947 is given in English translation in the appendix. The book makes profitable reading for high school and undergraduate students.
>
> JMH, Vol. 28, No. 4, p. 422.
> R: H. Gordon Skilling

318. CARTER, Gwendolen M. <u>Government of the Soviet Union.</u> New York, Harcourt, Brace & World, 1963. 181p. $2.25, paper.

> A reprint of Part II of the author's work <u>Major Foreign Powers</u>, containing a new 54-page section of seven Soviet constitutional documents. This title can be utilized by high school and college students as a handy reference source.

318a. CONQUEST, Robert, ed. <u>The Politics of Ideas in the U.S.S.R.</u> New York, Praeger, 1967. 176p. $5.25.

> This book traces the development of the organizations that bring all spheres of intellectual activity into conformity with the Communist Party's "general line"-among them the administration for literary and publishing affairs, the agency that controls plays and films, the centralized book distribution system, and the Central Committee's Department of Agitation and Propaganda.

319. CONQUEST, Robert. <u>Russia After Khrushchev.</u> New York, Praeger, 1965. 264p. $5.95.

A panoramic and sophisticated overview of
the Khrushchev era and its immediate aftermath as well as a thought-provoking discussio
of the many diverse factors likely to condition
future political developments in the USSR.
The author in his expectations is not optimis-
tic. This study merits thorough reading
and discussion.

EE, Vol. 15, No. 1, pp. 54-56.
R: Robert Bass

320.   FAINSOD, Merle. How Russia is Ruled. Cambridge,
Harvard University Press, 1953. 575p. $5.75.
(Russian Research Center Studies, No. 11) Rev.
ed. 1965. 698p. $9.50.

This book is of great interest to the general
reader who wants to inform himself about
Russian government, leadership, current
policies and economic organization. Be-
sides ample documentation, there is the
added illumination gained from the author's
interviews with many people who have lived
under Communist rule.

SR, Vol. 13, No. 3, pp. 439-40.
R: Philip W. Buck

321.   FAINSOD, Merle. Smolensk Under Soviet Rule.
Cambridge, Harvard University Press, 1958.
484p. $8.50; New York, Vintage Press. $2.45,
paper.

A highly important selection with interpretation of official files and records of the
Communist party of the Soviet Union for
the province of Smolensk. These sources
were captured by the German army in 1941.
The study reveals the methods of Soviet
dictatorship and shows the impact of
Stalinism on the local level as well as the
working of the intricate party machinery.
A basic title for library collections.

AHR, Vol. 64, No. 3, pp. 656-57.
R: John S. Reshetar, Jr.

322. FRIEDRICH, Carl J. and Zbigniew K. Brzezinski.
Totalitarian Dictatorship and Autocracy. Cambridge,
Harvard University Press, 1956. 346p. $4.25.
2nd ed.; Praeger, 1967. 448p. $9.95, cloth;
$2.95, paper.

> The theme of the study is debatable yet
> very enlightening since it illustrates the
> totalitarian political systems such as the
> Soviet government and its politics. The
> revised, enlarged edition shows many im-
> provements.

> SR, Vol. 16, No. 3, pp. 401-2.
> R: Philip W. Buck

322a. GRIPP, Richard C. Patterns of Soviet Politics.
Rev. ed. Homewood, Ill., The Dorsey Press,
1967. 386p. $8.00.

> Historical development of changing Soviet
> politics from its beginning to the present.

323. HAZARD, John N. The Soviet System of Government. Chicago, University of Chicago Press,
1957. 256p. 3rd ed., rev. and enlarged, 1964.
282p., cloth $5.50, paper $2.50.

> The author presents a summary of informa-
> tion about the Soviet system of government
> that is suitable for the beginning student
> and the general public.

> SR, Vol. 16, No. 3, pp. 394-95.
> R: H. Malcolm Macdonald

> SEEJ, Vol. 9, No. 2, p. 237.
> R: Ivan Taborsky

324. JUVILER, Peter H. and Henry W. Morton. eds.
Soviet Policy-Making: Studies of Communism in
Transition. New York, Praeger, 1967. 274p.
$6.50.

A panel of Sovietologists explore such areas as agriculture, industry, family life and contemporary morals and international relations. The contributors examine the ways important issues are determined and manipulated by the Party leadership and how the decisions are influenced by outside factors.

325.   KOESTLER, Arthur. Darkness at Noon. New York, New American Library, 1956. 188p. $1.12.

An outstanding work of literary penmanship based on the realities of Soviet life. Recommended for outside reading to stimulate a student's interest in the study of the Soviet Union.

326.   KULSKI, Wladyslaw W. The Soviet Regime. Syracuse, N.Y., Syracuse University Press, 1959. 524p. $8.00, cloth; $3.95, paper. 4th ed. 1963.

A substantial documentary account of political, social, economic and Party life in the USSR is contained in this lucid presentation. Indispensable reference work for students of Soviet affairs.

327.   LINDEN, Carl A. Khrushchev and the Soviet Leadership, 1957-1964. Baltimore, Johns Hopkins Press, 1966. 270p. $7.50.

After 1953 Kremlin politics assumed oligarchic tendencies, lacking constitutional checks and appeal to public opinion. As the consequence of this mysterious episode, Khrushchev never succeeded in eliminating all his rivals. He remained, as this account illustrates, first among equals.

EE, Vol. 16, No. 4, pp. 55-56.
R: George A. Lanyi

328.   McCLOSKY, Herbert and John E. Turner. The Soviet Dictatorship. New York, McGraw-Hill, 1960. 657p. $11.95.

This is the most comprehensive postwar
volume on the Soviet government system.
One-third of the book is devoted to an historical survey of the Marxist and Russian
backgrounds of Bolshevism, its growth and
triumph, together with a concise summary
of developments within the Communist
party, including Khrushchev's rise to power.
The text is difficult for the non-specialist,
however useful as a reference.

SR, Vol. 20, No. 2, pp. 317-20.
R: Peter H. Juviler

329. McNEAL, Robert H. The Bolshevik Tradition:
Lenin, Stalin, and Khrushchev. Englewood Cliffs,
N. J., Prentice-Hall, 1963. 181p. $1.95.

The author examines the development of the
Communist party in Russia under its three
leaders. The presentation is readable and
easily understood by students.

330. MOORE, Barrington, Jr. Soviet Politics: The
Dilemma of Power. Cambridge, Harvard University Press, 1950. 503p. $6.00.

The book features the historical development
of Soviet institutions and the issue of terror.
Decision-making, bureaucracy, promotion
of world revolution and national expansion,
collectivization, social stratification and
industrialization are scrutinized providing
plentiful material for discussions.

330a. NETTL, Paul J. The Soviet Achievement. New
York, Harcourt, Brace & World, 1967. 288p.
$3.95, paper.

An interpretation of the major changes and
developments in the USSR from 1917 to
1967. This volume traces the shifting
balance between theory and practice in the
government's application of Marxist theory
to practical problems.

331. PENKOVSKY, Oleg. The Penkovsky Papers.
Introduction and Commentary by Frank Givney.
Foreword by Edward Crankshaw. Translated by
Peter Deriabin. Garden City, N. Y., Doubleday,
1965. 411p. $5.95.

>Colonel Penkovsky revealed in this drama-
>tic account the life of the Soviet elite and
>inner cabinets. His testimony affords the
>reader a look into the life of the upper
>echelons of the Soviet society. Students
>should be urged to get acquainted with
>this source of information.
>
>JMH, Vol. 38, No. 2, pp. 236-38.
>R: Thomas W. Wolfe

331a. RAYMOND, Ellsworth. The Soviet State. New
York, Macmillan, 1968. 496p. $8.95.

>Soviet history, government, economics,
>and foreign policy are thoroughly examined
>in this comprehensive text. Special emphasis
>is given to World War II, Soviet propaganda,
>Soviet minorities, police, industrial mobili-
>zation for war and the Brezhnev-Kosygin
>regime.

332. RESHETAR, John S. Jr. Problems of Analyzing
and Predicting Soviet Behavior. New York,
Doubleday, 1955. 69p. $.95 (Doubleday Short
Studies in Political Science)

>The author surveys and evaluates the uses,
>abuses and disuses of the "ideological"
>and "cultural" approaches to Soviet conduct,
>various procedures for estimating Soviet
>capabilities and sundry Soviet source
>materials.
>
>SR, Vol. 15, No. 1, pp. 132-33.
>R: Frederick L. Shuman

333. RUSH, Myron. Political Succession in the USSR.
New York, Columbia University Press, 1965.
223p. $5.95.

An over-all analysis of the problems of
succession in the Soviet Union. The nature
of the Soviet society with its lack of a de-
fined procedure for political succession
gives rise to a succession crisis. This
is part of the price paid for the peculiar
role of the Communist party in the Soviet
state. The speculative nature of the topic
suggests plentiful material for discussion.

JMH, Vol. 38, No. 2, pp. 235-36.
R: Warren Lerner

334. SCHAPIRO, Leonard. The Government and Politics
of the Soviet Union. London, Hutchinson's, 1965.
191p.; Rev. ed.: New York, Random House, Vintage Books, 1965. 192p. $1.95.

This short handbook is designed to familiar-
ize students with political institutions of the
Soviet Union. The author goes to great
length to explain the principles on which the
Soviet political system is based. His lucid
and objective account is a model of succinct
summary and interpretation. Students and
teachers alike will appreciate this study.

SEER, Vol. 45, No. 104. pp. 260-61.
R: Merle Fainsod

335. SCOTT, Derek J. Russian Political Institutions.
New York, Holt, Rinehart and Winston, 1958.
265p. 3rd. ed., New York, Praeger, 1966.
276p. $7.00, cloth; $2.25, paper. (Praeger
Publications in Russian History and World
Communism, No. 94)

An undergraduate textbook introducing
students to the study of the Soviet system
of government. This book contains
encyclopedic information which is also
of great value to the teacher.

SR, Vol. 18, No. 2, p. 253.
R: John N. Hazard

336.   SWEARER, Howard R. with Myron Rush. The
        Politics of Succession in the U. S. S. R. Materials
        on Khrushchev's Rise to Leadership. Boston,
        Little-Brown, 1964. 324p. $2.95, paper.

> This is a documentary case history intend-
> ed primarily as an aid in college courses
> on Soviet politics. As such it should prove
> highly useful, but it will also be appreciated
> by both specialists in Soviet studies and the
> more general readers interested in contem-
> porary foreign politics. The core of the
> book consists of five chronologically
> arranged chapters covering the period from
> Stalin's death to Khrushchev's assumption
> of the premiership in March, 1958.

> SR, Vol. 25, No. 4, pp. 734-35.
> R: T. H. Rigby

337.   ULAM, Adam B. The New Face of Soviet Totali-
        tarianism. Cambridge, Harvard University Press,
        1962. 233p. $4.95. New York, Praeger, 1965.
        $1.95, paper. (Russian Research Center Studies,
        No. 47)

> The study consists of seven articles cover-
> ing a broad aspect of Soviet political life,
> including ideology, practical foreign and
> domestic politics, and intellectual deve-
> lopment. Valuable for courses in recent
> Soviet history.

> AHR, Vol. 70, No. 1, p. 255.
> R: Robert Paul Browder

338.   WOLFE, Bertram D. Communist Totalitarianism:
        Keys to the Soviet System. Rev. ed.: Boston,
        Beacon Press, 1961. 328p. $4.95.

> Discussed is the nature of Soviet power
> by one of the foremost Western experts.
> An important title in the field of Soviet
> affairs which students should be encouraged
> to study.

SR, Vol. 21, No. 4, pp. 757-59.
R: William B. Ballis

339. WOLFE, Thomas W. Soviet Strategy at the Cross-roads. Cambridge, Harvard University Press, 1964. 342p. $5.95.

> The author offers a wealth of information on Soviet defense policy in his analysis of the development of Soviet military policy and strategy since the Cuban crisis of October, 1962. The book is based on authoritative Soviet sources and is very suitable as reference for librarians and teachers.

> AHR, Vol. 70, No. 4, pp. 1207-8.
> R: Charles V. P. von Luttichau

340. WOLIN, Simon and Robert Slusser. The Soviet Secret Police. New York, Praeger, 1957. 408p. $8.00. (Research Program on the U.S.S.R. Series, No. 17).

> Significant study of a rather obscure but vitally important role of the political police. A compendium of materials relating to the history, structure, functions and activities of the security organ of the Soviet state.

> SR, Vol. 17, No. 4, pp. 540-42.
> R: Robert C. Tucker

S. Propaganda

341. BARGHOORN, Frederick C. Soviet Foreign Pro-paganda. Princeton, N.J., Princeton University Press, 1964. 329p. $6.00.

> Using the concepts developed by modern social scientists for the analysis of politi-cal communication, the author investigates

138

and reports on the role of propaganda in the conduct of Soviet foreign relations. Prof. Barghoorn compares the Soviet and Western approaches to international political communication and traces the general strategy of Soviet propaganda, using both Soviet and Western sources. This is a standard work on the subject.

342. BARGHOORN, Frederick C. The Soviet Image of the United States: A Study in Distortion. New York, Harcourt, Brace, for Yale Institute of International Studies, 1950. 297p. $4.00.

An interesting account surveying the Soviet propaganda picture of American wickedness from the early years to the Korean war. The book is not an analysis of propaganda techniques but rather a description of content, with excerpts and anecdotes.

SR, Vol. 10, No. 3, pp. 231-32.
R: Frederick L. Schuman

343. CLEWS, John C. Communist Propaganda Techniques. Foreword by G. F. Hudson. New York, Praeger, 1964. 236p. $8.50.

A discussion of the ideological and political contexture of Communist propaganda against a historical background. Lenin's doctrine of propaganda, modern use of mass communication, development of a Soviet propaganda organization, its role during Stalinist and post-Stalinist periods as an instrument of Soviet front organizations are described and evaluated.

SR, Vol. 25, No. 1, pp. 167-68.
R: Frederick C. Barghoorn

344. INKELES, Alex. Public Opinion in Soviet Russia: A Study in Mass Persuasion. Cambridge, Harvard University Press, 1950. 379p. $5.00: 2nd ed.

1958. 393p. $7.50. (Russian Research Center Studies, No. 1)

> A pioneering study in the methods of Soviet propaganda. The author placed particular emphasis on communication media since 1917 and their influence upon Soviet social life telling us how Russians behave and why they behave as they do.

> SR, Vol. 10, No. 2, pp. 146-47.
> R: Joseph Barnes

345. MICKIEWICZ, Ellen Propper. Soviet Political Schools: The Communist Party Adult Instruction System. New Haven, Yale University Press, 1967. 190p. $6.50. (Yale Russian and East European Studies, No. 3)

> This is the first examination of an indoctrination system that Khrushchev considered the most important component of internal propaganda and which his successors have placed at the highest levels of Communist Party activity. The author assesses the strengths and weaknesses of this hierarchy of institutions devoted to what Soviet sources call the "political tempering" of adults.

T. The Red Army and Militarism

346. ERICKSON, John. The Soviet High Command: A Military-Political History, 1918-1941. New York, St. Martin's Press, 1962. 889p. $15.00.

> A history of the origins and development of Soviet military leadership with an account of the relationship between the military and political rulers. Special attention is paid to the political administration of the armed forces and the commissars as well as the great purges within the army and the connec-

tion of military power and foreign policies. Though not easily read because of style and a multiplicity of minute detail, the publication nevertheless contains vital reference material.

AHR, Vol. 68, No. 4, p. 1065.
R: Warren B. Walsh

347.   GARDER, Michael. History of the Soviet Army. New York, Praeger, 1966. 226p. $7.50. (Praeger Publications in Russian History and World Communism No. 172)

This is an interpretative survey of the Soviet army's development. It is basically a summary account, and an interesting review of the Soviet armed forces. The Soviet army of today is the creation of the party, yet it is also firmly rooted in the Russian historical past.

EE, Vol. 16, No. 6, p. 52.
R: Raymond L. Garthoff

348.   GARTHOFF, Raymond L. ed. Soviet Military Policy: A Historical Analysis. New York, Praeger, 1966. 28 $6.50.

The book offers the first comprehensive analysis of present-day Soviet, Chinese and other Communist views and actions with respect to the relationship of war and revolution. Tracing the role of military power in Soviet society, ideology, and domestic and foreign policy, the author appraises the influence of the military in politics, technological developments, and the reorganization of the class structure within the Soviet Union. This book is recommended for students of Soviet affairs and also for the general reader.

348a.   KOLKOWICZ, Roman. The Soviet Military and the Communist Party. Princeton, N.J., Princeton

University Press, 1967. 448p. $9.00.

> Focusing mainly on the period since Stalin's death, the author tries to define the areas where the interests of Party and military coincide and those where they conflict. He also analyzes recent changes in the Soviet Union concerning the military establishment.

349. LIDDELL HART, Basil H. ed. The Red Army. New York, Harcourt, Brace and World. 1956. 480p. $6.00.

> A history of the Soviet army from its origins and an appraisal of its present state as seen through the eyes of some thirty collaborators of this volume. A single most valuable book on this topic in English, it is expected to be used as a reference source for years to come.

> JMH, Vol. 29, No. 3, pp. 278-79.
> R: Herbert S. Dinnerstein

350. Military Strategy: Soviet Doctrine and Concepts. Edited by Marshal V.D. Sokolovsky. Introduction by Raymond L. Garthoff. New York, Praeger, 1963. 416p. $6.50, cloth; $2.95, paper.

> Fifteen leading Soviet military theoreticians offer an exposition of the general concepts of strategy, warfare, and mobilization. The book itself is a revealing historical document.

U. Religion

351. ATTWATER, Donald. The Christian Churches of the East. Rev. ed. Vol. I: Churches in Communion with Rome. 232p. $7.50. Vol. II: Churches not in Communion with Rome. 260p. $7.50. Milwaukee, Bruce Publishing, 1961-62.

> This is an unpretentious work since the author has compiled data scattered in numerous publi-

cations, American and foreign, written in various languages. The style of the presentation is simple and it is easily understood.

SR, Vol. 22, No. 3, pp. 589-91.
R: N. S. Timasheff

352. FLETCHER, William C. comp. Christianity in the Soviet Union: An Annotated Bibliography and List of Articles; Works in English. Los Angeles, Research Institute on Communist Strategy and Propaganda, University of Southern California, 1963. 95p. $1.25.

588 entries, including a list of translations of articles from the Soviet press.

353. KOLARZ, Walter. Religion in the Soviet Union. New York, St. Martin's Press, 1961. 518p. $12.50.

Unlike most of the works on religion in Russia, this one deals not only with the Orthodox Church but also with all the other religious denominations in the USSR. In this regard it is the most complete study of the religious spectrum in the Soviet Union and a valuable source of information. This volume deserves a prominent place on the list of books designed for the study of the USSR.

SR, Vol. 22, No. 3, pp. 588-89.
R: Serge A. Zenkovsky

354. SPINKA, Matthew. The Church in Soviet Russia. New York, Oxford University Press, 1956. 162p. $3.50.

A report on the relations of the Russian Orthodox Church and the Soviet state. This small volume admirably answers many questions frequently asked on this topic.

JMH, Vol. 29, No. 3, p. 302.
R: Robert P. Browder

355. ZATKO, James J. Descent into Darkness: The
Destruction of the Roman Catholic Church in Russia,
1917-1923. Notre Dame, Ind., University of Notre
Dame Press, 1965. 232p. $6.95.

> An authoritative study on the systematic
> destruction of the Catholic Church in the
> Soviet Union, an event that has been
> scarcely publicized.

V. Social Conditions

356. ALLILUYEVA, Svetlana. Twenty Letters to a Friend.
Translated by Priscilla Johnson McMillan. New York,
Harper & Row, 1967. Russian, 216p. $8.50; English,
256p. $5.95.

> A dramatic story told by the daughter of the
> late dictator, Josef Stalin, about herself and
> her family's life in the Soviet Union during
> the Stalin regime. The Letters shed light on
> the Soviet society, its contexture and struggle
> for power and influence.

357. BLACK, Cyril E. ed. The Transformation of Russian
Society: Aspects of Social Change Since 1861. Cambridge, Harvard University Press, 1960. 695p.
$12.00.

> Publication of papers delivered by various
> specialists at Arden House in April, 1958.
> This unique volume defines a problem,
> poses a theory and suggests an approach.
> The collection has more value for advanced
> students of Russian history than for the
> beginner.
>
> SR, Vol. 20, No. 4, pp. 701-2.
> R: Robert F. Byrnes

358. DALLIN, David J. and Boris I. Nicolaevsky. Forced
Labor in Soviet Russia. New Haven, Yale University

Press, 1947. 331p. $3.75.

This study has yet to be surpassed by a new version. The authors discuss the development of the forced labor phenomenon in Soviet Russia, basing their account on Soviet and emigre sources, showing terrorist practices during the Stalin era. Informative reading for any student regardless of specialization.

359. FIELD, Mark G. Soviet Socialized Medicine: An Introduction. New York, Free Press, 1967. 231p. $6.95.

Analysis of the structure and method of working of the Soviet medical services. The author points out the advantages and shortcomings of the completely socialized medical field.

360. HINDUS, Maurice. The Kremlin's Human Dilemma: Russia After Half a Century of Revolution. Garden City, N.Y., Doubleday, 1967. 395p. $5.95.

A penetrating analysis of Soviet state power and the society, permitting a deeper look into the Soviet world. Recommended as additional reading material.

361. INKELES, Alex and Raymond A. Bauer. The Soviet Citizen: Daily Life in a Totalitarian Society. Cambridge, Harvard University Press, 1959. 533p. $10.00. (Russian Research Center Studies, No. 35)

The book resulted from examination of 3,000 questionaires filled out by refugees from the Soviet Union in connection with the Harvard Project on the Soviet Social System. A wide spectrum of issues of daily life is investigated. A historical record of great importance pertaining to the nature of the totalitarian Soviet state.

362. INKELES, Alex and Kent Geiger. eds. Soviet Society: A Book of Reading. Boston, Haughton Mifflin, 1961. 703p. $7.50.

Collection of seventy-three of the most
significant recent articles and documents
concerning Soviet society. A few articles
are taken directly from Soviet sources.
Suitable for sociology courses on the Soviet
Union as well as for offerings in other disciplines, the book will go far toward solving
the frustrating lack of periodicals in college
libraries and as such should be recommended
without hesitation.

SR, Vol. 21, No. 1, pp. 171-72.
R: Allen Kassof

363. MEHNERT, Klaus. <u>Soviet Man and His World</u>.
Translated from German by Maurice Rosenbaum.
New York, Praeger, 1962. 310p. $5.95, cloth;
$2.25, paper.

The author evaluates the impact of three
primary influences upon the present-day
Russian: his heritage of traditional Russian
characteristics, the forces of industrialization, and the pressures of Communist social
engineering.

SR, Vol. 22, No. 1, pp. 158-59
R: Edwin B. Morrell

W. <u>World War II</u>

364. CLARK, Alan. <u>Barbarossa</u>: The Russian-German
Conflict, 1941-45. New York, Morrow, 1965.
522p. $10.00.

A military study of combat operations on a
grand scale. Four major battles are the
pivot of this narrative: Moscow, 1941;
Stalingrad, 1942; Kursk, 1943; and the
Oder in 1945. Fascinating reading.

JMH, Vol. 37, No. 4, pp. 505-7.
R: Louis Morton

365. DALLIN, Alexander. German Rule in Russia, 1941-
1945. New York, St. Martin's Press, 1957. 695p.
$10.00.

> A detailed and systematic treatment of major
> aspects of German rule in the Soviet Union. A
> very enlightened discussion of German "Ost-
> politik." The bulk of the Nazi-dominated pop-
> ulation, with millions of non-Russians, were
> kept by Germans in a status which discouraged
> any national aspirations and even made the ma-
> ifestations of such aspirations punishable. A
> valuable contribution to the history of Eastern
> Europe during World War II.

> SR, Vol. 18, No. 3, pp. 443-45.
> R: Ihor Kamenetsky

366. GALLAGHER, Matthew P. The Soviet History of
World War II: Myths, Memories and Realities.
New York, Praeger, 1963. 205p. $6.50, cloth;
$1.95, paper. (Praeger Publications in Russian
History and World Communism, No. 121)

> This short and eminently readable book traces
> the fluctuations of the Soviet propaganda line
> in relation to World War II. The book, of
> interest to a wide scope of readers, uses a
> wealth of primary and secondary sources.

> AHR, Vol. 68, No. 4, pp. 1138-39.
> R: Edmond Masson

X. Youth

367. FISHER, Ralph Talcott, Jr. Pattern for Soviet
Youth: A Study of the Congresses of the Komsomol,
1918-1954. New York, Columbia University Press,
1959. 452p. $6.75. (Studies of the Russian Insti-
tute, Columbia University, No. 27)

> A pioneering study of the All-Union Leninist
> Communist League of Youth, the Komsomol
> congresses. The author illustrates the

pattern of attitudes and conduct that the Communist party sought to impose upon the Soviet youth comprising 17 million members as of 1953.

AHR, Vol. 65, No. 1, p. 181.
R: Arthur E. Adams

368. KASSOF, Allen. The Soviet Youth Program: Regimentation and Rebellion. Cambridge, Harvard University Press, 1965. 206p. $5.50. (Russian Research Center Studies, No. 49)

A methodical analysis of the organization and indoctrination of Soviet youth and of the regime's hectic attempt to achieve the socialization of this youth. The author points out that, despite de-Stalinization, there has been no basic change in the regime's commitment to achieve complete political indoctrination of the youth. The Soviet regime is not ready to tolerate liberalization.

JMH, Vol. 38, No. 2, p. 235.
R: Warren Lerner

Y. Research on the Soviet Union

368a. FISHER, Harold H. ed. American Research on Russia. Bloomington, Indiana University Press, 1959. 240p. $5.00.

A collection of 13 essays written by specialists in such areas as history, economics, philosophy and religion, social relations, science, literature, linguistics and other areas. The authors review the state of American research in these disciplines indicating possible topics which most urgently require further investigation. This book is the first major attempt to analyze the results of American studies on the Soviet Union since World War II, and is recommended for students of Soviet affairs.

368b. LAQUEUR, Walter. ed. <u>The State of Soviet Studies</u>.
Cambridge, Mass., M. I. T. Press, 1965. 177p.
$7.50.

The authors discuss the origins, present
state and goals of Soviet studies for the purpose of emphasizing their importance, advo-
cating greater expansion and diversity of
knowledge in this field, and encouraging
improved research in these areas.

CHAPTER III

NON-RUSSIAN SOVIET REPUBLICS

A. Belorussia

369. VAKAR, Nicholas P. Belorussia: The Making of a
      Nation - A Case Study. Cambridge, Harvard Uni-
      versity Press, 1956. 296p. $6.50. (Russian Re-
      search Center Studies, No. 21)

> A rare study dealing with a little known na-
> tion of Eastern Europe. Belorussian nation-
> alism revived only at the beginning of the
> twentieth century. The country's recent
> history is a fascinating and often horrifying
> case study in the interplay of nationalism
> and communism.
>
> JMH, Vol. 29, No. 2, pp. 172-73.
> R: Robert P. Browder

370. VAKAR, Nicholas P. Bibliographic Guide to Belo-
      russia. Cambridge, Harvard University Press,
      1956. 63p. $2.00.

B. Baltic States

371. BILMANIS, Alfred. A History of Latvia. Princeton,
      N.J., Princeton University Press, 1951. 441p.
      $6.00.

> This survey of Latvian history, the first in
> English, from its beginning to the time of
> Soviet annexation in 1940, explains the
> birth of national consciousness and quite

thoroughly covers the period of Latvian independence, 1920-1940.

SR, Vol. 11, No. 3, pp. 237-39.
R: Mabone W. Graham

372.   GIMBUTAS, Marija. The Balts. New York, Praeger, 1963. 286p. $6.95.

The fullest account of the history of the Balts that is available in English. A highly useful treatment for both the specialist and general reader with 79 photographs which convey a closer understanding.

SR, Vol. 24, No. 1, pp. 131-32.
R: Konstantinas Avizonis

373.   KIRCHNER, Walter. The Rise of the Baltic Question. Newark, University of Delaware Press, 1954. 294p. $4.50.

The author, in discussing the role which the eastern Baltic region played in world affairs, traces the history of sixteenth-century Livonia where international conflicts were decided. A pioneering work in English.

JMH, Vol. 28, No. 4, pp. 420-21.
R: C. Leonard Lundin

374.   MANNING, Clarence A. The Forgotten Republics. New York, Philosophical Library, 1952. 264p. $2.75.

A balanced account of the singular fate of the three Baltic nations, Estonia, Latvia and Lithuania, from the dawn of their history to their annexation by the Soviets in 1940. A still up-to-date reference source.

SR, Vol. 12, No. 4, pp. 572-73.

375.   NODEL, Emanuel. Estonia: Nation on the Anvil. New York, Bookman Associates, 1964. 207p. $5.00

The first English-language account of the struggle of the Estonian nation against Germanization and Russification from 1721 to 1940. Valuable aid to Baltic history.

SR, Vol. 24, No. 3, pp. 542-43.
R: Edgar Anderson

376. PAGE, Stanley W. The Formation of the Baltic States: A Study of the Effects of Great Power Politics Upon the Emergence of Lithuania, Latvia, and Estonia. Cambridge, Harvard University Press, 1959. 193p. $4.50.

This compact volume succeeds in analyzing and describing the events of 1917-1920 which enabled these nations to free themselves from Russian, German and Soviet bondage and to embark as sovereign states.

AHR, Vol. 65, No. 4, p. 901.
R: John H. Wuorinen

377. SENN, Alfred Erich. The Emergence of Modern Lithuania. New York, Columbia University Press, 1959. 272p. $6.00.

The study is considered the best English-language treatment of the modern development of Lithuania, a country that has played an important role in European history.

AHR, Vol. 65, No. 2, pp. 425-26.
R: Edgar Anderson

378. SENN, Alfred Erich. The Great Powers, Lithuania, and the Vilna Question, 1920-1928. Leiden, Netherlands, Brill, 1966. 329p. (Studies in East European History, No. 11)

The volume deals with the Lithuanians' struggle for independence, particularly their concern for Vilna, Lithuania's historical capital. The detailed account is of interest to advanced students of East European history.

AHR, Vol. 72, No. 4, p. 1383.
R: Stanley W. Page

379.   TARULIS, Albert N. American-Baltic Relations,
1918-1922: The Struggle Over Recognition. Washington, Catholic University of America Press, 1965.
386p. $8.95.

> Treatment of the Wilsonian self-determination
> policy on the example of the Baltic countries.
> The Baltic dissatisfaction with part of this
> policy is described dispassionately. A
> worthwhile study of a phase of American
> diplomacy and a good addition to the scanty
> literature of the Baltic area.

> SR, Vol. 25, No. 3, pp. 700-1.
> R: Edgar Anderson

380.   VARDYS, V. Stanley. ed. Lithuania under the
Soviets: Portrait of a Nation, 1940-1965. New
York-London, Praeger, 1965. 299p. $7.00.

> This useful compendium on Lithuania
> helps overcome the scarcity of needed
> sources in English. This book examines
> in particular the Soviet occupational policy
> in Lithuania.

> SR, Vol. 24, No. 3, pp. 543-44.
> R: Alfred Erich Senn

C.   Transcaucasia

381.   HOVANNISIAN, Richard G. Armenia on the Road
to Independence, 1918. Los Angeles, University
of California Press, 1967. 364p. $8.50.

> The book demonstrates that the establish-
> ment of the national Republic of Armenia in
> 1918 was sanctioned by the Armenian leaders
> in a desperate attempt to save the country
> from Russian Bolshevism and to salvage the

remnants of their people and the few districts still free of Ottoman occupation. A commendable study on a neglected topic.

382. KAZEMZADEH, Firuz. The Struggle for Transcaucasia, 1917-1921. Introduction by Michael Karpovich. New York, Philosophical Library, 1951. $5.75. Oxford, Ronald, 1951. 356p.

> The best detailed treatment thus far on the problem and history of small Transcaucasian nations: Armenia, Georgia and Azerbaidzhan. Recommended reading in courses of modern Russian history.

383. LANG, David M. The Last Years of the Georgian Monarchy, 1658-1832. New York, Columbia University Press, 1957. 333p. $5.50. (Studies of the Russian Institute, Columbia University)

> A history of one of the oldest states conquered by Russia and subjected to Russification and a gradual destruction of native culture and tradition.

384. LANG, David M. A Modern History of Soviet Georgia. New York, Grove Press, 1962; Praeger, 1963. 298p. $6.50.

> This study surveys the Soviet period of the Georgian republic and as such throws light on the problems of nationalities in the Soviet Union. Georgia's national independence of 1917-1920 was put to an end by Soviet Russian troops.

384a. NALBANDIAN, Louise Z. The Armenian Revolutionary Movement: The Development of Armenian Political Parties Through the Nineteenth Century. Berkeley, University of California Press, 1963. 247p. $6.00.

> The book, the first of its kind in English, describes the armed struggle of Armenian

rebels against the Ottoman Turks, ranging
from the first major uprising in 1863 to
the massacres of 1896.

D. Ukraine

1. Bibliographies and Encyclopedias

385. GREGOROVICH, Andrew. Books on Ukraine and
Ukrainians: A Selected Annotated List of 200 Books
in English, French, German and Spanish. Toronto,
Ukrainian National Youth Federation of Canada, 1964.
29p.

386. LAWRYNENKO, Jurij. Ukrainian Communism and
Soviet Russian Policy Toward the Ukraine: An
Annotated Bibliography, 1917-1953. Foreword by
John S. Reshetar. New York, Praeger, for Re-
search Program on the USSR, 1953. 454p. $4.75.

387. WERES, Roman. The Ukraine: Selected References
in the English Language. With Brief Introduction
about the Ukraine and Ukrainians. Kalamazoo,
Mich., School of Graduate Studies, Western Michigan University, 1961. 233p. $4.00.

388. Ukraine: A Concise Encyclopedia. Vol. I. Prepared by the Shevchenko Scientific Society. Edited
by Volodymyr Kubijovyc. Foreword by Ernest J.
Simmons. Toronto, University of Toronto Press,
1963. 1185p. $37.50.

> The most reliable and useful single-volume
> information on the Ukraine available in En-
> glish. Together with its forthcoming com-
> panion volume it will be an indispensable
> source for anyone interested in Ukrainian
> studies.

2. History and Historiography

389.　ADAMS, Arthur E.　Bolsheviks in the Ukraine:
The Second Campaign, 1918-1919.　New Haven,
Yale University Press, 1963.　440p.　$8.75.

> This is a most welcome addition to the
> meager number of studies on the Ukraine by
> Western scholars in comparison with the
> voluminous output on Russian topics.　The
> conquest of the Ukraine by Soviet Russia was
> made possible by the disunity of anti-Bolshe-
> vik groups and their failure to win peasant
> support.

> JMH, Vol. 37, No. 1, pp. 112-13.
> R:　David MacKencie

390.　The Annals of the Ukrainian Academy of Arts and
Sciences in the U. S., Vol. IX (1961), No. 1-2
(27-28).　Studies in History of the Post-Revolutionary
Ukraine and the Soviet Union.　New York, 344p.　$6.00.

> An excellent treatment of Soviet politics and
> its trend toward non-Russian nations of the
> USSR as illustrated on the example of the
> Ukraine, second in size and population
> among the Soviet republics.　The collection
> of articles, written by various specialists,
> are generally scholarly and informative.
> An appendix lists post-war doctoral disserta-
> tions on the Ukraine in West European and
> American universities.

> SR, Vol. 22, No. 2, pp. 339-40.
> R:　Basil Dmytryshyn

391.　The Annals of the Ukrainian Academy of Arts and
Sciences in the U. S., Vol. V-VI (1957), No. 4-1,
2.　Special Issue.　A Survey of Ukrainian Historiography by Dmytro Doroshenko; Ukrainian Historiography 1917-1956 by Olexander Ohloblyn.　New
York, 1957.　456p.　$6.00.

> This is a work of unusual value to the
> serious student of Eastern European
> studies, for it not only provides a con-

venient and detailed outline of the development of Ukrainian historiography but also includes a vast bibliographical apparatus.

SR, Vol. 18, No. 1, pp. 123-24.
R: John S. Seshetar, Jr.

392.   ARMSTRONG, John A. Ukrainian Nationalism.
New York, Columbia University Press, 1955. 322p.
2nd ed. 1963. 361p. $7.50.

An exhaustive study of the modern Ukrainian national phenomemon which was and still is in the position to challenge seriously Communist dictatorship in the Ukraine. The study is extensively documented providing a wealth of material for the study of nationalism in the Soviet Union. The second edition includes a chapter on the struggle of the Ukrainian Insurrection Army (UPA) against the Soviet regime in the Ukraine from 1945 to 1950.

JMH, Vol. 28, No. 4, pp. 404-6.
R: George Fischer

SR, Vol. 23, No. 4, pp. 771.
R: John S. Reshetar, Jr.

393.   BILINSKY, Yaroslaw. The Second Soviet Republic:
The Ukraine after World War II. New Brunswick,
N. J., Rutgers University Press, 1964. 539p.
$12.50.

The author examines the Ukrainian national development in terms of key criteria and issues. A general introductory chapter deals with the principal characteristics of the period and is followed by an extensive treatment of the industrial demographic and socio-economic bases of Ukrainian nationalism. Linguistic Russification has been stressed, too, in this sophisticated study illuminating the relations of nationalities in the USSR.

AHR, Vol. 70, No. 4, pp. 1111-12.
R: John S. Reshetar, Jr.

394.   BORYS, Jurij. The Russian Communist Party and
the Sovietization of Ukraine. Stockholm, The Author,
1960. 374p.

> A well documented account of Russian-Ukrain-
> ian relations in the critical years 1917-1923.
> An examination of the Communist doctrine
> of self-determination of nations as it per-
> tained to the Ukraine. An excellent biblio-
> graphy included.

395.   DMYTRYSHYN, Basil. Moscow and the Ukraine,
1918-1953. New York, Bookman Associates, 1956.
310p. $5.50.

> The principal emphasis of this book is on
> the attitudes and high policy decisions of
> the Communist Party in the Ukraine. After
> tracing in brief outline the Bolshevik nation-
> ality theory, the author precedes to a de-
> tailed description of Soviet policies in the
> Ukraine in the 1920's. Also included are
> such topics as the place occupied by the
> Ukraine in the Soviet economy, agreements
> between Moscow and Kiev and the composition
> of the Communist Party of the Ukraine.

> SR, Vol. 17, No. 1, pp. 123-24.
> R: Richard Pipes

396.   HRUSHEVSKY, Michael. A History of Ukraine.
Edited by O.J. Frederiksen. Preface by George
Vernadsky. New Haven, Yale University Press,
1941. 629p. $5.00.

> This volume from his "Short History of
> Ukraine" represents the only translation
> of any of Hrushevsky's works and can well
> serve as textbook and as general reference
> source.

397.　KAMENETSKY, Ihor.　Hitler's Occupation of the Ukraine, 1941-1944. Milwaukee, Marquette University Press, 1956.　101p.　$3.00 (Marquette Slavic Studies, No. 2)

> In a survey of Nazi planning for the occupation of the Ukraine, Hitler was determined to turn the country into a German colony in which the Ukrainian population would be reduced to serfdom.
>
> SR, Vol. 16, No. 3, pp. 411-12.
> R:　John A. Armstrong

398.　KONONENKO, Konstantyn.　Ukraine and Russia: A History of Economic Relations Between Ukraine and Russia, 1654-1917. Milwaukee, Marquette University Press, 1958.　257p.　$6.50. (Marquette Slavic Studies, No. 4)

> The Ukraine's natural resources made her vulnerable to economic exploitation and the victim of Russian colonialism.　The Soviet regime continues to follow the tsarist example of investing less than taking from the Soviet Ukraine.

399.　KOSTIUK, Hryhory.　Stalinist Rule In the Ukraine: A Study of the Decade of Mass Terror, 1929-1939 New York, Praeger, 1960.　162p.　$4.95. (Published for the Institute for the Study of U.S.S.R.)

> Dispassionate description of Stalin's terror in the Ukraine.　The book contains valuable information on the purges and is useful for the study of history of the Ukraine under Soviet rule.

400.　MANNING, Clarence A.　Hetman of Ukraine: Ivan Mazeppa. New York, Bookman Associates, 1957.　234p.　$3.50.

> The only English-language study of the foremost Ukrainian hetman.　A balanced treatment of Mazeppa who, in alliance with King

Charles XII of Sweden, led the unsuccessful war against Russia. The account elucidates the Russo-Ukrainian conflict.

401. MANNING, Clarence A. The Story of the Ukraine. New York, Philosophical Library, 1947. 326p. $3.75.

This is primarily an account of the relations of the Ukraine to Russia. It is lucidly composed and suitable for the general reader.

SR, Vol. 6, Nos. 18-19, pp. 183-84.
R: Oliver J. Frederiksen

402. NAHAYEWSKY, Isidore. History of Ukraine. Philadelphia, America Publishing House, 1962. 295p. $5.00.

A concise popular historical account of the Ukrainian people from the dawn of their existence to the present, with special emphasis on religious life.

SR, Vol. 22, No. 3, pp. 559-60.
R: Robert S. Sullivant

403. PIDHAINY, Oleh S. The Formation of the Ukrainian Republic. Preface by M. Mladenovic. Toronto, New Review Books, 1966. 685p. $10.75. (The Ukrainian Republic in the Great East-European Revolution, Vol. I)

A description of how the Ukrainian statehood was brought about in 1917-1918. The author concludes that the Ukraine had "consolidated its sovereignty, had completed its period of formation and entered as an equal into the world community of states." An exhaustively documented treatment.

AHR, Vol. 72, No. 4, pp. 1451-52.
R: Arthur E. Adams

404. RESHETAR, John S., Jr. The Ukrainian Revolution,

1917-1920: A Study in Nationalism. Princeton, Princeton University Press, 1952. 363p. $5.00.

> An important title of East European litera-
> ture on a crucial period. The author has
> prepared a sound treatment of this particu-
> lar topic. The movement of nationalism is
> traced from its origins in the mid-nineteenth
> century to the ultimate collapse of the
> Ukrainian national state in 1920.
>
> SR, Vol. 12, No. 1, pp. 145-47.
> R: William Korey

404a. STACHIW, Matthew. Ukraine and Russia. Translated from Ukrainian by Walter Dushnyck. New York,
Ukrainian Congress Committee of America, Inc.,
1967. 215p. $4.00.

> The book covers the period from 1917 to
> 1918 when the Ukrainian struggle for inde-
> pendence took place, giving a thorough pic-
> ture of the Russian aggression against
> Ukraine from the vantage point of an eye
> witness.

405. VERNADSKY, George. Bohdan Khmelnytsky, Hetman
of Ukraine. New Haven, Yale University Press, 1941
150p. $2.50.

> A biography of the most prominent figure of
> the Ukrainian Cossacks whose leader led the
> fight against the Poles. Khmelnytsky founded
> the Cossack state in the middle of the seven-
> teenth century.

406. YAREMKO, Michael. Galicia-Halychyna: From
Separation to Unity. With an introduction by
Clarence A. Manning. Toronto-New York-Paris,
Shevchenko Scientific Society, 1967. 292p. $7.00.
(Shevchenko Scientific Society, English Section,
Vol. 3)

> A rather popular history of Galicia, the
> first of its kind in English, from the

beginning through 1945. The national claims of Ukrainians, the historical aspirations of the Poles and Soviet domination after World War II involve Western Ukraine, as Galicia is also known. An extensive bibliography serves both the specialist and the student.

3. Government and Politics

407. ARMSTRONG, John A. The Soviet Bureaucratic Elite: A Case Study of the Ukrainian Apparatus. New York, Praeger, 1959. 174p. $6.50.

> Minute details about Soviet bureaucrats. Moving constantly between Communist Party and Soviet state, these bureaucrats created an elite open freely at the bottom but confined at the top to individuals who were catapulted to responsibility to replace seniors purged by Stalin.

> SR, Vol. 19, No. 1, pp. 117-18.
> R: John N. Hazard

407a. KOLASKY, John. Education in Soviet Ukraine. Toronto, Peter Martin Associates, 1968. 238p. $5.00, cloth; $3.50, paper.

> The book presents for the first time a close analysis of Russian cultural and ethnic nationalism within the Soviet Union. The author's well-documented study denounces Soviet claims about the generosity of Russian treatment of minority cultures within the Soviet Union. The book is essential reading for educators, students of the Soviet Union and Communism, and everyone interested in the rights of ethnic and linguistic minorities.

408. SULLIVANT, Robert S. Soviet Politics and the Ukraine, 1917-1957. New York-London, Columbia

University Press, 1962. 438p. $8.50.

Pioneering research on the nature of Soviet nationalities policy as manifested in the second largest Soviet republic, Ukraine. The book's considerable value lies in its character as a broad survey of events that are little known in the Western world.

SR, Vol. 23, No. 1, pp. 146-47.
R: Arthur E. Adams

PART II

EASTERN EUROPE — GENERAL

1. Handbooks

409.   ISENBERG, Irvin, et al. The Soviet Satellites of Eastern Europe: An Introduction to the Geography, History, Peoples and Problems of the Soviet-Dominated Nations of Eastern Europe. New York, Scholastic Book Services, 1963. 160p. $0.65, paper. (Scholastic World Affairs Multi-Text, No. 3)

General introduction into the East European area, primarily for secondary schools. Its simple style and wide range of subjects and geographic area is best suited for the beginning student.

SR, Vol. 24, No. 1, pp. 161-63.
R: John M. Thompson

2. Bibliographies

410.   The American Bibliography of Slavic and East European Studies. Bloomington, Indiana University Publications. Slavic and East European Series, annual vols. 1957-. $3.50 per vol.

A useful serial limited to materials in the
English language.

411. BYRNES, Robert F. Bibliography of American Publications on East Central Europe, 1945-1957. Bloomington, Indian University Publications, 1958. 213p.
$2.50. (Slavic and East European Series, Vol. 12)

This collection is of particular service to
advanced students without foreign language
competence.

412. LENCECK, Rado L. A Bibliographical Guide to the
Literature on Slavic Civilizations. New York,
Columbia University, Department of Slavic Languages,
1966. 52p. $2.00.

413. Newspapers of East Central and Southeastern Europe
in the Library of Congress. By the Reference Department, Library of Congress. Washington, Govt. Printing Office, 1965. 204p. $1.00.

A list of Library of Congress holdings of 787
newspapers published since World War I.

414. A Select Bibliography: Asia, Africa, Eastern Europe,
Latin America. New York, American Universities
Field Staff, 1960. 534p. $4.75. Supplement, 1961.
75p. Sections Russia and the Soviet Union, pp. 257-
324, East Central Europe, pp. 325-353.

415. U. S. Library of Congress. Slavic and Central Euro-
pean Division. The USSR and Eastern Europe:
Periodicals in Western Languages. Edited by
Robert G. Carlton. Washington, The Library of
Congress, 1965. 204p. $ 0.45.

3. General Works

416. BORSODY, Stephen. The Triumph of Tyranny:
The Nazi and Soviet Conquest of Central Europe.

New York, Macmillan, 1960. 285p. $4.50

This highly stimulating book combines political history with a political program. It displays in detail the fascinating and tragic picture of internecine political infighting among the smaller powers of Central and East Europe since they achieved independence as a result of World War I.

SR, Vol. 20, No. 2, pp. 313-315.
R: Aleksander W. Rudzinski

417. KERTESZ, Stephen D. ed. East Central Europe and the World: Development in the post-Stalin Era. Notre Dame, Ind., University of Notre Dame Press, 1962. 386p. $6.50.

Fourteen specialists analyze developments which occurred in all East European countries, including East Germany, since 1953, revealing the complexity of inherent issues of this part of Europe. Highly recommended to students of international affairs.

417a. LONDON, Kurt, ed. Eastern Europe in Transition. Baltimore, The Johns Hopkins Press, 1966. 364p. $3.45.

The work is a symposium of 14 discussion papers selected from among those presented at the Fifth International Conference held in September, 1965, in Noordwijk, Holland. Topics deal with political, ideological, and social behavior of East European societies and their relations to the western world. The authors agree that the Sino-Soviet dispute affected in a decisive manner the status of the Eastern European states and parties, greatly enhancing their chances of achieving independence from Moscow and strengthening their centrifugal tendencies.

EEQ, Vol. 1, No. 4, pp. 416-19.
R: V. Benes

418.   SINGLETON, Frederick B. Background to Eastern
       Europe. Oxford-New York, Pergamon Press, 1965.
       226p. $3.75.

              An overall introduction into the history, econ-
              omy and political conditions of the East Euro-
              pean countries. The handbook-like treatment
              of various aspects renders this publication
              suitable for general reference.

419.   U. S. Congress. House. Committee on Foreign
       Affairs. Recent Developments in the Soviet Bloc.
       Hearings before the Subcommittee on Europe. 88th
       Congress, 2nd Session. Washington, U. S. Govt.
       Printing Office. 1964. 2 Parts. 390p. $0.45 and
       $0.55 respectively.

              A general review of recent trends in Soviet
              and East European literature, arts, human
              rights, law, religion, youth, economic
              developments, political trends, implications
              for U. S. foreign policy, distribution of
              American publications and State Department
              views. All persons appearing before the
              Subcommittee are specialists in Soviet bloc
              affairs.

       4.   Communism

420.   BROMKE, Adam and Philip E. Uren. eds. The
       Communist States and the West. New York, Prae-
       ger, 1967. 256p. $6.50, cloth, $2.25, paper.

              Twelve essays describe and evaluate changes
              in the Communist world in terms of East-
              West relations. Covered are such questions
              as power versus ideology, alliance struc-
              tures and international equilibrium. The
              book succeeds in conveying to the beginning
              student something of the new international
              reality.

421. BURKS, R. V. The Dynamics of Communism in Eastern Europe. Princeton, Princeton University Press; London, Oxford University Press, 1961. 244p. $5.00, cloth; 1961. $2.95, paper.

   An analytical history of Communist parties in East European countries. The author explains the different forms of Communist activities prior to seizure of power. A pioneer study on this subject.

422. BUZEK, Antony. How the Communist Press Works. New York, Praeger, 1964. 287p. $7.50.

   A description of the working of newspapers and press, agencies in the Soviet Union, and East European satellites, illustrating the distinct characteristics of journalists of these countries. There is a list of all major newspapers and periodicals of the Soviet bloc.

   JMH, Vol. 37, No. 2, pp. 281-82.
   R: Richard Wortman

423. DANIEL, Hawthorne. The Ordeal of the Captive Nations. Introduction by Harold R. Medina. New York, Doubleday, 1958. 316p. $4.50.

   A needed survey of events which took place in East Europe, the Baltic States and the Balkan during and immediately after World War II and the Communization of this large area.

424. SKILLING, H. Gordon. Communism National and International: Eastern Europe After Stalin. Toronto, University of Toronto Press, 1964. 168p. $4.95, cloth; $1.95, paper.

   Refreshing discussion of Communism and its encounter of local nationalism in the examples of East European countries. The book stimulates interest for further reading and student discussion.

SR, Vol. 24, No. 2, pp. 337-38.
R: John C. Council

5. Comecon

425. KASER, Michael. Comecon: Integration Problems of
the Planned Economics. London-New York, Oxford
University Press, 1965. 215p. $5.60.

The author examines the many aspects of
Comecon in terms of cooperation and
diversity of interests among the individual
member-countries.

6. Foreign Relations

425a. BYRNES, Robert F. ed. The United States and
Eastern Europe. Englewood Cliffs, N.J. Prentice
Hall, 1967. 179p. $4.95, cloth; $1.95, paper.
(The American Assembly, Columbia University)

A collection of essays, authored by various
specialists, appraising United States relations with the countries of Eastern Europe.

426. CAMPBELL, John C. American Policy Toward
Communist Eastern Europe: The Choices Ahead.
Minneapolis, University of Minnesota Press, 1965.
136p. $4.50.

Evaluation of the political situation as it
exists in contemporary East European
countries, stressing the approaches the
United States has to consider in regard to
these countries. With sound judgment the
various alternatives at the diplomatic,
cultural, economic and military levels are
pointed out. Excellent for political science
courses.

SR, Vol. 25, No. 3, pp. 547-49.
R: Josef Korbel

427. MAMATEY, Victor S. The United States and East Central Europe, 1914-1918. A Study in Wilsonian Diplomacy and Propaganda. Princeton, Princeton University Press, 1957. 431p. $10.00.

This book explores various facets of Wilsonian diplomacy in the latter part of the First World War. It discusses the aims and aspirations of ethnic groups in the Danubian area, the Czechs and Slovaks, the Southern Slavs and the Rumanians. Broad in its conception and sound in its conclusion.

JMH, Vol. 30, No. 3, pp. 263-64.
R: Otakar Odlozilik

428. WANDYCZ, Piotr S. France and Her Eastern Allies, 1919-1925. French-Czechoslovak-Polish Relations from the Paris Peace Conference to Locarno. Minneapolis, University of Minnesota Press, 1962. 454p. $8.50.

The author examines a three-way diplomatic relationship that both reflected and contributed to the ambiguous and uncertain international scence in the years immediately following the Versailles settlement. The implications of Locarno had little to offer to encourage the brighter future of this part of Europe.

SEEJ, Vol. 7, No. 2, p. 234.
R: Henry L. Roberts

7. Geography

429. OSBORNE, R. H. East-Central Europe: An Introduction to Geography. New York, Praeger, 1967. 384p. $7.50, cloth; $2.95, paper.

An up-dated introductory textbook on the
geography of East-Central Europe. Individual chapters deal with the land, climate,
soils, land use and farming, industry and
mining, population and principal cities,
transport and trade. Fifty maps and a
detailed bibliography make this work indispensable for high school and college libraries.

430. Oxford Regional Economic Atlas of USSR and Eastern
Europe. 2nd ed. London, Oxford University Press,
1960. 134p. $10.00.

The most comprehensive English-language
atlas to date. An excellent tool for teacher
and student.

431. POUNDS, Norman J. G. ed. Geographical Essays
on Eastern Europe. Bloomington, Indiana University Press, 1961. 159p. $4.00. (Russian and East
European Series, No. 24)

8. Economy and Economic Conditions

432. KARCZ, Jerzy F. ed. Soviet and East European
Agriculture. Berkeley, University of California
Press, 1967. 445p. $10.00 (Russian and East
European Studies).

A collection of essays discussing the trends
in manpower, the role of women in Soviet
agriculture, Khrushchev's impact on Soviet
farming and socialized agriculture in
Czechoslovakia.

433. SPULBER, Nicholas. The Economics of Communist
Eastern Europe. New York, The Technology Press
of M.I.T. and Wiley, 1957. 525p. $12.50.

This volume is still an up-to-date basic textbook, primarily on the graduate level. It

is also highly recommended as a comprehensive handbook of factual information
based on impressive literature of Communist and Western sources.

SR, Vol. 18, No. 1, pp. 117-19.
R: Victor H. Winston

434. SPULBER, Nicholas. The State and Economic
Development in Eastern Europe. New York, Random House, 1966. 179p. $3.95.

Three essays on the economic conditions
of East European countries. The author,
who pioneered with numerous publications
about this neglected area, has presented a
dark picture of the state of economy under
Communism.

EE, Vol. 16, No. 7, p. 58.
R: L. A. D. Dellin

9. History

435. BROWN, J. F. The New Eastern Europe: The
Khrushchev Era and After. New York, Praeger,
1966. 306p. $6.50, cloth; $2.25, paper.

The author treats the history of Eastern
Europe since 1956 by individual countries,
describing political, economic, cultural
and diplomatic events. Well written, this
book is probably the best single effort of this
kind since the publication of Seton-Watson's
East European Revolution in 1951.

SR, Vol. 26, No. 2, pp. 326-28.
R: R. V. Burks

436. BURKS, Richard V. Some Elements of East European History. Washington, Service Center for
Teachers of History, 1961. 26p. $0.50.

Brief evaluation of the most critical and important aspects of East European history. A selected and partly annotated bibliography for extensive reading is helpful to the instructor and student.

437. CROSS, Samuel H. Slavic Civilization Through the Ages. Edited with a foreword by Leonid Strakhovsky. Cambridge, Harvard University Press, 1948. 195p.

A brief outline of Slavic history and culture which can be used by the beginner on high school and college level.

438. DVORNIK, Francis. The Slavs in European History and Civilization. New Brunswick, N. J., Rutgers University Press, 1962. 688p. $15.00.

This impressive work treats the political, constitutional, social, and cultural history of the region between the Baltic, Adriatic, and Black seas. It is a continuation of the author's The Slavs, Their Early History and Civilization (Boston, 1956) and, to some extent, of his The Making of Central and Eastern Europe (London, 1949). The volume provides an excellent index and a unique bibliography which renders it a useful reference work. The book belongs in a basic collection of Slavica in any library.

SR, Vol. 22, No. 3, pp. 547-48.
R: Imre Boba

439. FISCHER-GALATI, Stephen. ed. Eastern Europe in the Sixties. New York-London, Praeger, 1963. 239p. $6.00, cloth; $2.25, paper.

Collaborative attempt of eight historians, economists, and political scientists to explain and analyze conditions in Eastern Europe. Through a variety of topics this reader provides a good picture of this area in the early 1960's.

SR, Vol. 24, No. 1, pp. 139-40.
R: James F. Clarke

440. FISCHER-GALATI, Stephen. ed. Twentieth Century
Europe: A Documentary History. Philadelphia,
Lippincott, 1967. 416p. $3.95, paper.

> This collection of significant documents,
> speeches, treaties, and other like material
> reflects the historical process which led
> to the current division of Eastern and
> Western Europe. The documents from
> Soviet and East European sources include
> the Rapacki Plan and Khrushchev's anti-
> Stalin address to the Twentieth Congress
> of the CPSU.

441. HALECKI, Oscar. Borderlands of Western Civilization: A History of East Central Europe. New
York, Ronald Press, 1952. 503p. $6.00.

> The author telescopes into this volume the
> significant events in the life stream of the
> various national identities of this area
> along with the politics of churches and
> empires, and the repercussions between
> Eastern and Western Europe occasioned
> by the periodic shift in the balance of
> power in either of both divisions. It can
> be used as a textbook and important refer-
> ence source.

> SR, Vol. 12, No. 1, pp. 147-49.
> R: Bruce C. Hopper

442. HALECKI, Oscar. From Florence to Brest (1439-
1596). Rome, Sacrum Poloniae Millennium; New
York, Fordham University Press, 1959. 449p.
$6.00.

> A history of endeavors wanting to achieve
> a union between the Western and Eastern
> churches in the Ruthenian lands of the
> Jagiellonian Commonwealth. A significant

contribution to this history of the Eastern church.

SR, Vol. 20, No. 2, pp. 523-27.
R: Ihor Sevcenko

443.   KOHN, Hans. Pan-Slavism: Its History and Ideology. Notre Dame, Ind., University of Notre Dame Press, 1953. 356 p. 2nd rev. ed: New York, Vintage Books, 1960. 468p. $1.95, paper.

The first comprehensive English-language survey of the pan-Slavic ideology. Pan-Slavism, originated among the Slavs, became an instrument of Russia's foreign policy. This study is highly provocative and enlightening. It is highly recommended for all types of libraries and to the student.

SR, Vol. 12, No. 3, pp. 419-21
R: Michael B. Petrovich

444.   MACARTNEY, C. A. and A. W. Palmer. Independent Eastern Europe: A History. London, Macmillian. New York, St. Martin's Press, 1962. 499p. $12.00; Reprint 1966. $4.95, paper.

This is mainly a history of Eastern European states between the two World Wars, a period during which the nations in that area formed sovereign national states on the ruins of large supranational empires: Turkey and the Austro-Hungarian Monarchy. The account is reliable and most useful for students of East European affairs.

SR, 23, No. 1, pp. 147-49.
R: Stephen D. Kertesz

445.   ROTHSHILD, Joseph. Communist Eastern Europe. New York, Walker, 1964. 168p. $4.50.

An analytical attempt of describing postwar events in Eastern Europe, this book

is of additional value containing appropriate reference addenda on East European
population, territory, national minorities,
Communist press, parties and leadership,
and economic development. Recommended
for outside reading to promote discussion
on the question of contemporary history.

SR, Vol. 25, No. 3, pp. 547-48.
R: Josef Korbel

446. SETON-WATSON, Hugh. East European Revolution. 3rd ed. New York, Praeger, 1955. 435p.
$6.50, cloth; $2.50, paper. (Praeger Publications
in Russian History and World Communism)

This is still the most readable survey of
East Europe, covering the years 1941-1949.
It concentrates on Poland, Czechoslovakia,
Hungary, Rumania, Bulgaria, Albania,
Yugoslavia, and Greece, describing gradual
Communization of these countries. Its
enormous bulk of factual information makes
it virtually a handbook of East Europe.

SR, Vol. 11, No. 2, pp. 153-54.
R: Ellsworth Raymond

447. SETON-WATSON, Hugh. Eastern Europe Between
the Wars, 1918-1941. Cambridge University Press,
1945. 442p. 21 s; New York, Macmillan, $6.50;
3rd ed.: Hamden, Conn., Shoe String Press, 1963.
$10.00.

This survey of East Europe during the inter-
war period is a precurser to the author's
The East European Revolution and is regarded
as an excellent textbook.

448. WARRINER, Doreen. ed. Contrasts in Emerging
Societies: Readings in the Social and Economic
History of South-Eastern Europe in the Nineteenth
Century. Selected and translated by G. F. Cushing,
E. D. Tappe, V. de S. Pinto, and Phyllis Anty.

Bloomington, Indiana University Press, 1965.
402p. $6.75.

A collection of readings of social and economic history pertaining to Hungary, Rumania,
Bulgaria, and the principal components of
what is now Yugoslavia. The selections include a wide variety of contemporary materials drawn from official sources, the works
of native reformers and accounts by travel-
ers.

JMH, Vol, 38, No. 1, pp. 88-89.
R: John C. Adams

10. Government and Politics

449. BENES, Vaclav, Andrew Gyorgy, and George Stambuk.
Eastern European Government and Politics. New
York, Harper & Row, 1966. 247p. $3.50, paper.

The authors treat contemporary governments
and politics of Czechoslovakia, East Germany,
Hungary, Poland, Rumania and Yugoslavia.
They explain successfully the development
and structure of individual Communist parties,
the problem of leadership and relations with
the Soviet Union since World War II. Recommended as an undergraduate textbook.

450. BRZEZINSKI, Zbigniew. The Soviet Bloc: Unity and
Conflict - Ideology and Power in the Relations among
the USSR, Poland, Yugoslavia, China and other Communist States. With an introduction by Robert R.
Bowie. Cambridge, Harvard University Press, 1960.
470p. $7.75; Revised and enlarged ed.: New York,
Praeger, 1967. 565p. $2.95, paper.

A solid analysis of the intricate relations within the Soviet bloc. The central theme is the
role of ideology and power in the Communist
orbit. This work is challenging to both instructor and student.

SR, Vol. 20, No. 1, pp. 123-25.
R: Stephen D. Kertesz

451.   KAMENETSKY, Ihor.   Secret Nazi Plans for Eastern
Europe: A Study of Lebensraum Policies.   New York,
Bookman Associates, 1961.   236p. $5.00.

>A scholarly study of the expansionist plans
>of National Socialism.   This book is particu-
>larly useful for its analysis of the geographic
>patterns of German colonization in Eastern
>Europe and for its emphasis on the scope of
>differential treatment of subject nationalities
>in the eastern regions; e.g., Baltic, Belo-
>russian and Ukrainian groups.

>AHR, Vol. 67, No. 3, pp. 785-86.
>R; Robert Koehl

452.   SKILLING, H. Gordon.   The Government of Communist East Europe.   New York, Crowell, 1966.   256p.
$2.50, paper.

>This book presents a first-class description
>of the Communist governments of Eastern
>Europe.   The study is careful, learned, well-
>written, and skillfully organized.   It will serve
>as a successful text for courses in governments
>of the area and as a handy reference.

>SR, Vol. 26, No. 2, pp. 326-28
>R: R. V. Burks

11.   Social Conditions

453.   CARLTON, Richard K. ed.   Forced Labor in the
"People's Democracies."   New York, Praeger, Pub-
lished for the Mid-European Studies Center of the
Free Europe Committee, 1955.   248p. $3.00.
(Praeger Publications in Russian History and World
Communism, No. 29)

>This collective work covers the legal frame-
>work of forced labor in the so-called "socialist

countries", the administration and the opera-
tion of the forced labor system. The impact
of de-Stalinization upon this aspect of socialist
structures is also discussed.

CHAPTER III

BALKAN PENINSULA — GENERAL

---

1. General Works

454. HOFFMAN, George W. The Balkans in Transition.
Princeton, N. J. Van Nostrand, 1963. 124p. $1.45,
paper.

> This study refers to the three countries that
> form the basic core of Southeastern Europe:
> Albania, Bulgaria, and Yugoslavia. The
> author discusses the geographical setting,
> the peoples of the peninsula, the evolution
> of the political-geographical factors that
> have contributed to the transition in the
> Balkans. Recommended for high school use.

2. History

455. ANDERSON, M. S. The Eastern Question. New
York, St. Martin's Press, 1966. 475p. $9.50.

> A history of the Ottoman empire during its
> last 150 years and its disintegration into
> national states. This study clarifies many
> aspects of nationalism in the Balkans.

456. COLES, Paul. The Ottoman Impact on Europe: 1350-
1699. New York, Harcourt, Brace & World, 1968.
216p. $2.95, paper.

> A study of the era of Ottoman power and its
> influence on the development of Europe. It
> offers an analysis of two cultures in the pro-
> cess of conflict, interpenetration and change.

457. DEIJER, Vladimir. The Road to Sarajevo. New
York, Simon & Shuster, 1966. 550p. $11.95.

> An excellent study, combining much scatter-
> ed information and throwing new light on the
> various problems of the Southern Slavs. It
> provides a broad historical background and
> tells of the many secret societies of the
> Bosnians. It describes how the assassins of
> Francis Ferdinand smuggled their arms from
> Serbia and how funds were obtained from
> Russia to pay the assassins. The author
> maintains that Pasic, the premier of Serbia,
> knew of the plot but failed to warn Vienna.
>
> SR, Vol. 26, No. 2, pp. 322-23.
> R: E. C. Helmreich

458. JELAVICH, Charles and Barbara Jelavich, eds.
The Balkans. Englewood Cliffs, N.J., Prentice-
Hall, 1965. 148p. $4.95.

> A brief survey of the complex history of the
> Balkans. The authors contend that national-
> ism has imposed a history of conflicts upon
> the area together with repeated interventions
> by great powers. The study may serve as a
> good introduction to more extensive study of
> the Balkan peoples.
>
> SR, Vol. 25, No. 3, pp. 547-48.
> R: Josef Korbel

459. JELAVICH, Charles and Barbara Jelavich, eds.
The Balkans in Transition: Essays on the Development of Balkan Life and Politics Since the Eighteenth
Century. Berkeley, University of California Press,
1963. 451p. $8.50.

> Thirteen essays analyze developments com-
> mon to the Balkans as a whole. This volume
> represents a valuable addition to the neglect-
> ed field of Balkan studies.
>
> SEEJ, Vol. 8, No. 3, pp. 352-53.
> R: Stephen Fischer-Galati

460.   SETON-WATSON, Robert William.   The Rise of
       Nationality in the Balkans.   London, Constable,
       1917.   308p.   Reprint: New York, Fertig, 1967.
       $8.50.

                This account, the most authoritative work in
                English on the historical evolution of the
                Balkan nations, begins with the period of
                Turkish hegemony and continues through
                the national struggles for independence in
                the nineteenth century, the Berlin Settle-
                ment and the Balkan Wars.

461.   STAVRIANOS, Leften S.   The Balkans, 1815-1914.
       New York, Holt, Rinehart and Winston, 1963.
       135p. $2.75, paper.   (Berkshire Studies in Euro-
       pean History)

                Condensed nineteenth-century history of the
                Balkans with emphasis on the national
                awakening of the Southern Slavs.   The brief
                presentation and readability make this book-
                let an ideal text for high schools.

462.   STAVRIANOS, Leften S.   The Balkans since 1453.
       New York, Holt, Rinehart and Winston, 1958.   970p.
       $14.50.

                This work is much more than a textbook; it
                makes available in a summary form mono-
                graphic material otherwise inaccessible
                even to most specialists.   The author has
                included a multilingual annotated bibliography
                so rich in material that it can be regarded
                as a most valuable aid for further study.

                SEER, Vol. 39, No. 92, pp. 253-54.
                R: V. J. Parry

463.   WOLFF, Robert Lee.   The Balkan in Our Time.
       Cambridge, Harvard University Press and London,
       Cumberlege, 1956.   618p. $8.00 (Russian Research
       Center Studies, No. 23)   New York, Norton, 1967.
       618p. $2.95, paper.

This volume is divided into two main sections: events before 1939 and the years 1939 to 1955. Four countries are introduced to the reader: Yugoslavia, Albania, Rumania and Bulgaria. Its simple and unpretentious style makes this study suitable for both high school and college students.

SEER, Vol. 39, No. 92, pp. 281-82.
R: V. J. Parry

CHAPTER IV

EASTERN EUROPE BY COUNTRIES

A. Albania

464.   SKENDI, Stavro. ed. Albania. New York, Published
for the Mid-European Studies Center of the Free
Europe Committee, Inc., by Praeger, 1956. 389p.
$7.50.

> A handbook that is designed for the general
> reader and for reference use which, in the
> case of Albania, is profiting the specialist
> and librarian as well with its broad scope
> and voluminous factual detail. The work
> includes biographical data of twenty-seven
> leading Communists, a brief chronology for
> 1944-55, a list of treaties and an impressive
> bibliography.

465.   SKENDI, Stavro. The Albanian National Awakening,
1878-1912. Princeton, N. J., Princeton University
Press, 1967. 498p. $13.75.

> The author, a native of Albania, traces the
> progress and setbacks of Albanians in their
> long history and struggle for national unity.
> Recommended as a college textbook.

> SR, Vol. 26, No. 4, pp. 680-82.
> R: Marin Pundeff

466.   HAMM, Harry. Albania - China's Beachhead in
Europe. Translated from German by Victor Anderson. New York, Praeger, 1963. 176p. $4.95.

The eminent German political journalist
produced an unpretentious yet illuminating
study. The author discusses the immediate
antecedents of Tirana's "revolt" against
Moscow, the factors behind Hoxha's decision to support the Chinese in the Sino-Soviet
dispute and the role and significance of the
Albanian issue at the Soviet Party's Twenty-
second Congress.

467. GRIFFITH, William E. Albania and the Sino-Soviet
Rift. Cambridge, M.I.T. Press, 1963. 423p. $7.95,
cloth; $2.95, paper.

In addition to a short history of Albania, the
author gives a careful analysis of the primary
causes of the rift between Moscow and Tirana.
Since books on Albania are rarely published
in English these days, the author has missed
an opportunity by aiming his study toward the
advanced student rather than the general
public.

SR, Vol. 23, No. 1, pp. 158-60.
R: T. Zavalani

B. Bulgaria

468. DELLIN, L.A.D. ed. Bulgaria. New York, Published for the Mid-European Studies Center of the Free
Europe Committee, Inc. by Praeger, 1957. 457p.
$8.50.

A collection of 1,243 items of general reference; land and people, language and literature,
history, politics, government and law.

SEER, Vol. 44, No. 103, pp. 529-30.
R: A. Helliwell

469. MacDERMOTT, Mercia. A History of Bulgaria,
1393-1885. New York, Praeger, 1962. 354p. $8.75.

In absence of a better English-language
history of Bulgaria, this one is to be recommended despite some obvious faulty analyses
and interpretations. The information on the
liberation movement is both new and relevant.

AHR, Vol. 68, No. 2, 528-29.
R: Stephen Fischer-Galati

470. ROTHSCHILD, Joseph. The Communist Party of
Bulgaria, Origins and Development 1883-1936. New
York, Columbia University Press, 1959. 354p. $7.5(

A noteworthy book, displaying a high standard
of scholarship in a lucidly written account of
the historical development of Socialism-Com-
munism in the Balkans.

SR, Vol. 20, No. 1, pp. 144-46.
R: William G. Vettes

C. Czechoslovakia (including Bohemia and
Slovakia)

1. Bibliographies and Handbooks

471. BOHMER, Alois. et al. Legal Sources and Bibliography of Czechoslovakia. New York, Praeger, 1959.
180p. $6.00. (Praeger Publications in Russian
History and World Communism, No. 19)

472. BUSEK, Vratislav and Nicholas Spulber. eds.
Czechoslovakia. New York, Published for the Mid-
European Studies Center of the Free Europe Com-
mittee, Inc., by Praeger, 1957. 520p. $10.00.

This handbook concentrates on four major
topics: geography and demography, the
Party and the government, the society, and
the economy. An appendix contains biographical sketches of leaders of the post-war regime

a brief chronology and a list of treaties and
agreements from 1943 to 1956.

JMH, Vol. 31, No. 1, pp. 68-69.
R: S. Harrison Thomson

2. Communism

473. KORBEL, Josef. Communist Subversion of Czechoslovakia, 1938-1948: The Failure of Coexistence.
Princeton, N. J., Princeton University Press, 1959.
258p. $5.00, cloth; $2.95, paper.

> A former member of the diplomatic service
> of Czechoslovakia describes the instruments
> of power seized by the Communist Party, its
> clever propaganda designed to convince the
> people of the moderation of its policies and the
> illusions to which the democrats fell victims.
> The author's first-hand experiences add to the
> book's importance.
>
> SEER, Vol. 39, No. 92, pp. 277-78.
> R: H. Seton-Watson

474. TABORSKY, Edward. Communism in Czechoslovakia
1948-1960. Princeton, N. J., Princeton University
Press, 1961. 628p. $12.50.

> Focused on the post-1948 period, this penetrating
> study offers a clear insight into the operation
> of a modern welfare-garrison state, in which
> people still have not learned to like Communism;
> they have merely learned to live under it. The
> book also portrays a unique aspect of people who
> are living under a totalitarian regime as "split
> personalities."
>
> SR, Vol. 21, No. 3, pp. 558-59.
> R: Ivo D. Duchacek

475. ZINNER, Paul E. Communist Stategy and Tactics in
Czechoslovakia, 1918-1948. New York-London, Praeger,

1963. 264p. $6.50.

The Communist seizure of Czechoslovakia still ranks high among the fateful events of the Cold War. This particular study has longevity as a standard treatment of the event as it substantially contributes to our understanding of why the Communists emerged victorious in a country that used to be regarded as a "bastion of democracy" in East Central Europe.

SR, Vol. 23, No. 2, pp. 352-53.
R: Edward Taborsky

3. Economy and Economic Conditions

476. MICHAL, Jan M. Central Planning in Czechoslovakia. Stanford, Stanford University Press, 1960; London, Oxford University Press, 1961. 274p. $5.75.

A critical evaluation of the economic growth in Czechoslovakia after the Communist takeover of 1948. In comparison with Western free enterprise, the Czechoslovak economy roughly equalled its output per capital but only by employing strict regimentation and great sacrifices, according to the author's findings.

4. Foreign Relations

477. LUZA, Radomir. The Transfer of the Sudeten Germans: A Study of Czech-German Relations, 1933-1962. With a Foreword by A. William Salomone. New York, New York University Press, 1964. 365p. $7.50.

An in-depth case study of majority-minority relationships and their effect on world peace.

The book is a genuine work of scholarship, clear and factual. It conveys to the reader a better understanding of the settlement of Munich and the expulsion of Germans from Czechoslovakia after World War II.

JMH, Vol. 37, No. 3, pp. 418-19.
R: Oscar I. Janowsky

5. History

478. KAMINSKY, Howard. A History of the Hussite Revolution. Berkeley, University of California Press, 1967. 580p. $15.00.

The religious reformation begun by John Huss in fifteen-century Bohemia was also a social, political and cultural revolution. The author maintains that the religious reformation and the socio-political revolution were inseparably connected and shows the significance of each thread.

479. LETTRICH, Jozef. History of Modern Slovakia. New York, Praeger, 1955. 329p. $5.00.

The book provides a brief sketch of Slovak history before 1918 and principal trends in Slovak politics and events during the first Czechoslovak Republic. The greater part of the study, however, is devoted to events since 1938 when; as a result of the Munich verdict, Czechoslovakia disintegrated and Slovakia was set up as a German protectorate. The author favors the so-called "Czechoslovak idea" as a solution to the Czech-Slovak relationship. Especially valuable are forty-one documents, most of which are printed in English for the first time.

JMH, Vol. 28, No. 1, p. 103.
R: Victor S. Mamatey

480. PERMAN, Dagmar Horna. The Shaping of the
Czechoslovak State: Diplomatic History of the
Boundaries of Czechoslvakia, 1914-1920. Leiden,
Netherlands, Brill, 1962. 339p. (Studies in East
European History, No. 7)

> The dissolution of the Habsburg Empire and
> the consequent rise of the successor states
> were accompanied by many frontier problems.
> This book examines the manner in which the
> Paris Peace Conference reached the decision
> fixing newborn Czechoslovakia's frontiers in
> the winter of 1918-1919. The author's scholar
> and objective treatment is especially noteworth
> An excellent bibliography aids the book's usefu
> ness.

> AHR, Vol. 69, No. 3, p. 844.
> R: Curt F. Beck

481. SETON-WATSON, Robert W. A History of the Czech
and Slovaks. London, 1943; Reprint: Hamden, Conn.
The Shoe String Press, 1965. 413p. $10.00.

> Standard history of Czech and Slovak peoples.
> Recommended for college libraries.

482. THOMSON, S. Harrison. Czechoslovakia in Europea
History. Princeton, N. J., Princeton University
Press, 1953. 485p. $7.50. Rev. ed.: Hamden,
Conn., Archon Books, 1965. 485p. $11.00.

> The best short history of Czechoslovakia in
> the English language. New chapters have
> been added or were re-written (on Munich)
> in the new edition, in order to utilize materi-
> al, mainly documents, from the Nuremberg
> Trials and from the files of the German
> Foreign Office. The author also up-dated
> the history to 1948.

> SR, Vol. 13, No. 2, pp. 277-78.
> R: Edward Taborsky

D. Hungary

1. General Works

483. HELMREICH, Ernest C. ed. Hungary. New York,
Published for the Mid-European Studies Center of
the Free Europe Committee, Inc., by Praeger,
1957. 466p. $8.50.

> Despite obvious discrepancies in all volumes
> of the series, this particular volume has not
> yet been made obsolete by a better reference
> book on Hungary. It contains a valuable sum-
> mary of what Communism has imposed on
> Hungary.

> SR, Vol. 17, No. 4, pp. 558-59.
> R: Joseph S. Roucek

2. Foreign Relations

484. KERTESZ, Stephen D. Diplomacy in a Whirlpool:
Hungary Between Nazi Germany and Soviet Russia.
Notre Dame, Ind., University of Notre Dame Press,
1953. 273p. $4.75.

> A very valuable book treating the diplomatic
> history of Hungary during the last years of
> the Horthy regime and the Turbulent time
> following World War II. As a former Hungarian
> diplomat, the author relates some of his person-
> al experiences during that time.

3. History

485. Free Europe Committee. The Revolt in Hungary:
A Documentary Chronology of Events Based Exclu-
sively on Internal Broadcasts by Central and Pro-
vincial Radios, October 23, 1956 - November 4,

1956. New York, Free Europe Committee, 1956. 112p. $1.00.

> The most reliable collection of original sources concerning the Hungarian revolution of 1956.

486. Hungary Today. by the Editors of Survey. New York, Praeger, 1962. 104p. $4.50.

> This volume consists of articles most of which were authored by Hungarian scholars in exile and originally published in the English periodical Survey. The book offers a remarkably perceptive portrait of the artificially revived but still shellshocked Hungarian Communist regime. The master theme running through the volume is the traumatic effect of the October Revolution of 1956.
>
> SR, Vol. 22, No. 2, pp. 338-39.
> R: Paul Kecskemeti

487. LASKY, Melvin J. ed. The Hungarian Revolution: The Story of the October Uprising as Recorded in Documents, Dispatches, Eye-Witness Accounts, and World-Wide Reactions. New York, Praeger, 1957. 318p. $5.00.

> This documentation of the Hungarian Revolt is a successful attempt to "catch history on its wings." The collection is prefaced by Hugh Seton-Watson's brilliant short essay on "Hungary 1945-1956." It shows a small nation, crushed by the East, and abandoned by the West, in its heroic struggle for freedom.
>
> SR, Vol. 18, No. 1, pp. 126-28.
> R: Stephen Borsody

488. LETTIS, Richard and William E. Morris, eds. The Hungarian Revolt. New York, Scribner, 1961. 219p. $1.95.

A compilation of reports, broadcasts, com-
mentaries, essays and excerpts from books
on the Hungarian Revolt. There are extensive excerpts from broadcasts by Hungarian
radio stations during the uprising.

489.   MACARTNEY, C. A. Hungary: A Short History.
Chicago, Aldine Publishing Co. , 1962. 262p. $4.50.

This short survey succeeds admirably in re-
counting all that is relevant in the long history of Hungary: from Arpad, who led the
Hungarians westward, to Janos Kadar, who
led them, after their latest heroic bid for
freedom in 1956, back to their prison of the
East. A smoothly flowing style, rich illustrations and maps enhance the work's
value for the lay reader.

490.   SINOR, Denis. History of Hungary. New York,
Praeger, 1959. 310p. $6.00.

This is chiefly a political history of Hungary.
Although highly condensed, the book reads
well. The interpretations are stimulating
though controversial in some instances. The
author presents the Hungarian point of view
on many issues of the past.

SR, Vol. 20, No. 3, pp. 531-32.
R: Stephen Borsody

491.   TÖKÉS, Rudolf L. Béla Kun and the Hungarian
Soviet Republic. Published for the Hoover Institu-
tion on War, Revolution and Peace. New York,
Praeger, 1967. 272p. $7.50.

The author provides the first comprehensive
survey of the social, political, and ideological origins of the Communist party of Hungary. Drawing on newly available sources,
he describes how Béla Kun declared a Soviet
Republic in Hungary in 1919, and how it fell
133 days later.

492. VALI, Ferenc A. Rift and Revolt in Hungary: Nationalism Versus Communism. Cambridge, Harvard University Press, 1961. 590p. $9.75.

> The most comprehensive study of the Hungarian Revolution to date. A well documented and judiciously balanced analysis of the institutional, societal, personal, and international background of the Revolution. The study of the clash between nationalism and Communism eventually turned out to be a concise history of the political, economic, and cultural-ideological changes caused by twelve years of Soviet and Communist domination in Hungary. An excellent source for the study of Communism on the example of an individual East European country following World War II.
>
> SR, Vol. 21, No. 2, pp. 353-54.
> R: George Barany

493. ZINNER, Paul E. Revolution in Hungary. New York, London, Columbia University Press, 1962. 380p. $6.00.

> An excellent treatment on the Hungarian thaw and revolution. Exhaustive in analysis, replete with psychological and sociological insight, and well balanced in judgment. It should be read by all students of Communism and of Central and Eastern Europe. The book is contemporary history, emphasizing analysis rather than chronological detail. The author has fully utilized the 10, 000 pages of Columbia University's Hungarian refugee interview project material.
>
> SR, Vol. 22, No. 1, pp. 165-66.
> R: William E. Griffith

E. Poland

1. General Works

494. BARNETT, Clifford R. et al. Poland: Its People, Its Society, Its Culture. New Haven, Conn., HRAF Press, 1958. 471p. $7.50. (Survey of World Cultures)

> This study presents all aspects of Polish society, politics, culture, and economy in their mutual interrelation and in their entirety. It is a source of information on Poland for the general public and may serve as a textbook for high school and undergraduate use.
>
> SR, Vol. 18, No. 3, pp. 467-70.
> R: Aleksander W. Rudzinski

495. HALECKI, Oscar. ed. Poland. New York, Publ. for the Mid-European Studies Center of the Free Europe Committee, Inc., by Praeger, 1957. 601p. $10.00.

> Twenty different chapters cover a variety of topics such as the land, the people, education, government, economic background, in addition to biographies, a brief chronology (1943-1956), and a bibliography. Some shortcomings do no great harm to this general reference tool.
>
> JMH, Vol. 30, No. 2, pp. 158-59.
> R: Joseph S. Roucek

2. Communism

496. DZIEWANOWSKI, M. Kamil. The Communist Party of Poland: An Outline of History. Cambridge, Harvard University Press, 1959. 369p. $7.50.

(Russian Research Center Studies, No. 32)

This is a valuable contribution to a field
of history which, until recently, has been
badly neglected: socialism and communism
in Eastern Europe, outside of Russia. The
study traces the history of the Polish socialist and communist movements and of the
respective parties, from their beginning in
the nineteenth century until the October
Revolution of 1956.

AHR, Vol. 67, No. 4, pp. 1109-1110.
R: Victor S. Mamatey

3. Foreign Relations

497. BUDUROWYCZ, Bohdan. Polish-Soviet Relations,
1932-1939. New York, London, Columbia University Press, 1963. 229p. $6.00.

The book conveys a sufficiently objective
picture of Polish-Soviet relations in these
fateful years. The author's account of the
years preceding the Polish war disaster
leaves no doubt that its rulers were extremely shortsighted men. The volume
aids the understanding of European diplomacy and may be used for class discussion.

SEER, Vol. 63, No. 100, pp. 245-47.
R: L. Blit

498. DEBICKI, Roman. Foreign Policy of Poland, 1919-
1939. From the Rebirth of the Polish Republic to
World War II. With a Foreword by Oscar Halecki.
New York, Praeger, 1962. 192p. $5.50.

A short and effective treatment of the complexity of Poland's foreign policy of the
inter-war period. The author's personal
experience of Polish diplomatic activity

conveys a deeper understanding of the matter. Students of international relations will find this study one of the best English-language presentations.

SR, Vol. 24, No. 2, pp. 339-40.

499. DRZEWIENIECKI, Walter M. The German-Polish Frontier. Chicago, Polish Western Association of America, 1959. 166p. $3.00.

A study of German-Polish past and contemporary relations, outlining an historical background and focusing on the post-World War II situation.

JMH, Vol. 32, No. 4, p. 434.
R: Kenneth F. Lewalski

500. HORAK, Stephan. Poland's International Affairs, 1919-1960: A Calendar. Bloomington, Indiana University Press, 1964. 248p. $6.50. (Russian and East European Series, Vol. 31)

This volume attempts to furnish valuable reference material of modern Polish history by listing almost all bilateral treaties to which Poland was a signatory between 1919-1960, including selected multilateral treaties and documents related to Poland in the same period.

SEEJ, Vol. 9, No. 3, p. 356.
R: Josef Korbel

501. KORBEL, Josef. Poland Between East and West: Soviet and German Diplomacy Toward Poland, 1919-1933. Princeton, N. J., Princeton University Press, 1963. 321p. $6.50, cloth; $2.95, paper.

Well-documented study on Polish diplomacy which found itself between two unfriendly and strong neighbors. A useful contribution to European diplomacy after World War II. The book also elaborates on the shortsightedness of Polish policy in not exploiting the German-Russian differences.

SR, Vol. 23, No. 4, pp. 771-73.
R: A. Romer

4. Geography

502. POUNDS, Norman J. G. Poland Between East and West. Princeton, N. J., Van Nostrand, 1964. 132p. $1.45, paper. (Van Nostrand Searchlight Book, No. 22)

> A critical evaluation of Polish history against her geographical location and neighborhood of two big powers, Germany and Russia. The author examines the period between the two World Wars; reviews the economic pattern of modern Poland under the Communist regime; and discusses the nation's subsequent history after World War II.

> SR, Vol. 24, No. 3, pp. 554-55.
> R: Huey Louis Kostanick

5. History

503. GIBNEY, Frank. The Frozen Revolution: A Study in Communist Decay. New York, Farrar-Straus-Cudahy, 1959. 264p. $4.75.

> This book is an example of an exceptionally successful journalistic research of events which took place in Poland in 1956. Since these events still await a scholarly treatment, this publication takes its place as an explanation of the situation of post-war Poland.

SR, Vol. 19, No. 4, pp. 606-607.
R: Richard F. Staar

504.   HALECKI, Oscar. A History of Poland. London,
Dent, 1942. 359p.; 2nd enlarged ed.: New York,
Roy, 1955. 373p. $3.95.

> A one-volume history of Poland, originally
> in Polish and now translated. Recommend-
> ed as a textbook on the undergraduate level
> as the best survey presentation. The new
> edition has been up-dated to 1955.

505.   HEYMANN, Frederick G. Poland and Czechoslovakia. Englewood Cliffs, N. J., Prentice-Hall, 1966.
181p. $4.95, cloth; $1.95, paper. (The Modern
Nations in Historical Perspective)

> Chronicling Poland's and Czechoslovakia's
> history from the Middle Ages to the present,
> the author examines recent developments in
> these nations, now a part of the Soviet bloc,
> in the light of their rich national heritage.
> This readable version will introduce students
> into the complex situation that has prevailed
> in this part of Europe.
>
> AHR, Vol. 72, No. 4, p. 1444.
> R: Otakar Odlozilik.

506.   HISCOCKS, Richard. Poland: Bridge for the Abyss?
An Interpretation of Developments in Post-War Poland.
London-New York-Toronto, Oxford University Press,
1963. 359p. $8.00.

> A notable presentation of events in Poland
> after World War I. The author portrays an
> accurate picture of Polish Communism from
> its beginning to its successful seizure of
> power with the help of the Russian Red Army
> in 1944-45. Despite some unjustified
> optimistic views, the book as a whole
> serves to illuminate Polish history follow-
> ing World War II.

SR, Vol. 23, No. 4, pp. 771-73.
R: A. Romer

507. KAPLAN, Herbert H. The First Partition of Poland.
New York-London, Columbia University Press, 1962.
215p. $5.00.

> A valuable and erudite work presenting
> unbiased discussion of the causes of the
> first partition of Poland. The subject is one
> that has divided Polish historians for over
> a century: were the partitions the result
> of Poland's chaotic political system, or
> were they the result of her neighbor's
> rapacity and greed? Mr. Kaplan bridges
> both interpretations.

> EE, Vol. 12, pp. 51-52.
> R: Eugene Kusielewicz.

508. KARBONSKI, Stefan. Fighting Warsaw. New York,
Funk & Wagnalls, 1967. $6.00, cloth; $2.95,
paper.

> A history of the German occupation of Poland
> during World War II written by the leader of
> the Polish underground movement.

509. KARSKI, Jan. The Story of a Secret State. Boston,
Houghton Mifflin, 1944. 318p. $3.00.

> A first-hand account of the Polish political
> and military underground movement which
> challenged German occupation during World
> War II. An excellent report on the nature
> and function of the underground movement.

510. KOMARNICKI, Titus. Rebirth of the Polish Republic:
A Study in the Diplomatic History of Europe, 1914-19·
Melbourne-London-Toronto, Heinemann, 1957. 776p.
$10.75.

> This remarkable account describes in detail
> the aspects of the Polish problem against
> the background of European diplomacy. An

advanced student of international affairs will greatly benefit from this study of diplomatic activity that resulted in the rebirth of the Polish state.

SR, Vol. 17, No. 2, pp. 247-49.
R: Oscar Halecki

511. ROTHSCHILD, Joseph. Pilsudski's Coup d'Etat. New York-London, Cambridge University Press, 1966. 435p. $10.00.

This is a major contribution to the modern history of Poland and Eastern Europe as well. In simple, understandable terms the author records and explains a highly complex metamorphosis of Polish political life which produced Pilsudski's coup d'etat in 1926. The book is recommended for those interested in modern European history and East European affairs in particular.

CSS, Vol. 1, No. 2, pp. 313-14.
R: Edgar Anderson

512. ROZEK, Edward J. Allied Wartime Diplomacy: A Pattern in Poland. New York, Wiley, 1958. 481p. $8.50.

This volume traces the story of Poland from the "fourth partition" in 1939, through the uneasy Stalin-Sikorski agreement of July, 1941, to the rupture of relations in March, 1943; the discussions at Teheran and Yalta; the Soviet sponsorship of the Lublin Committee and the tortuous efforts at a lop-sided compromise between the "Lublin" and "London" Poles; and finally the period of Mikolajczyk's participation in the new government of "national unity". A piece of thorough and mature reflection, this book stands out by its painstaking and frequently novel documentation.

SR, Vol. 18, No. 2, pp. 265-66.
R: Alexander Dallin

513. STAAR, Richard F. Poland, 1944-1962: The Sovietization of a Captive People. Baton Rouge, Louisiana State University Press, 1962. 300p. $7.50.

> In absence of a superior treatment of Polish
> post-war history, this book deserves the
> attention of readers in search of factual in-
> formation on contemporary Poland. The
> Polish case among the captive nations has
> been attracting the interest of students of
> East European affairs more than the other
> countries.

SR, Vol. 22, No. 3, p. 556.
R: M. K. Dziewanowski

514. ZAWODNY, Janusz K. Death in the Forest: The
Story of the Katyn Forest Massacre. Notre Dame,
Ind., University of Notre Dame Press, 1962. 235p.
$6.50.

> A very important document of Soviet crime
> committed on thousands of Polish prisoners
> of war in the Katyn Forest near Smolensk.
> At least 4,500 bodies were found. Prof.
> Zawodny has painstakingly examined every
> available scrap of documentary information,
> displaying his findings dispassionately and
> convincingly.

SR, Vol. 23, No. 1, pp. 153-55.
R: Paul E. Zinner

6. Minorities

515. HORAK, Stephan. Poland and Her National Minorities, 1919-1939. New York, Vantage Press, 1961.
259p. $5.00.

The author illustrates how the Polish government treated the thirty per cent non-Polish population of the re-emerged Polish state, comprising the ethnic groups of Belorussians, Germans, Jews, Lithuanians and Ukrainians. The book stresses the severe educational, economic and colonizing measures which the Polish government employed.

JMH, Vol. 34, No. 4, pp. 462-63.
R: Stanley W. Page

7. Politics and Government

516. BROMKE, Adam. Poland's Politics: Idealism vs. Realism. Cambridge, Harvard University Press, 1967. 316p. $9.95. (Russian Research Center Studies, No. 51)

> The traditional gap between idealism and realism in Polish politics is the object of the author's labor of research and definition. He examines the program and the policies of the Communist party and other political movements in a broad historical perspective in order to achieve a better understanding of the contemporary Polish political development.

> EE, Vol. 16, No. 6, pp. 49-51.
> R: Alexander Bregman

F. Rumania

1. Bibliographies and Handbooks

517. FISCHER-GALATI, Stephen A. ed. Rumania. A Bibliographic Guide. Washington, Slavic and Central European Division, Ref. Dept., Library

of Congress, 1963. 75p. $0.45.

SR, Vol. 23, No. 4, pp. 792-93.
R: Glenn Torrey

518. FISCHER-GALATI, Stephen A. ed. Romania.
New York, Publ. for the Mid-European Studies
Center of the Free Europe Committee, Inc., by
Praeger, 1957. 399p. $8.50.

General reference material on Rumania
comprising the government and the Party,
literature and the arts, economy and history. A sound addition to professional
literature.

SR, Vol. 18, No. 2, p. 268.
R: Andrew Gyorgy

2. Communism

519. IONESCU, Chita. Communism in Rumania, 1944-
1962. London, Oxford University Press, 1964.
378p. $8.00.

A history of the Rumanian Communist Party
since its inception in 1921 and of its post-
war administration in particular. The author
examines not only events but also the national
interpretation of events when "the Party has
become its own historian." Because of its
chronological arrangement this book is
easily understood by the beginner and the
lay reader.

SEER, Vol. 64, No. 102, pp. 250-52.
R: M. C. Kaser

3. Foreign Relations

520. JELAVICH, Barbara. Russia and the Rumanian
National Cause, 1858-1859. Bloomington, Indiana

University Press, 1959. 169p. $4.00. (Slavic and East European Series, Vol. 17)

> This detailed and thoroughly documented monograph is primarily based on the private papers and official reports of Nikolai K. Giers, who served as the Russian consul general in Bucharest from 1859 to 1863. There is an excellent introductory chapter on Russia and the Principalities from 1829-1858.

> JMH, Vol. 32, No. 3, p. 299.
> R: E. C. Helmreich

4. Economy

521. ROBERTS, Henry L. Rumania: Political Problems of an Agrarian State. New Haven, Yale University Press, 1951. 414p. $6.00.

> This work offers a very thorough analysis of Rumania's economic and political history during the past thirty years. The author's study of the Rumanian peasant's unsuccessful struggle is, in most of its findings, equally valid for other agricultural societies throughout East Europe. From this point of view this study maintains its importance, even today, in view of the similarity of conditions in Africa, South America and Asia.

> SR, Vol. 21, No. 2, pp. 159-61.
> R: David Avram

522. MONTIAS, John M. Economic Development in Communist Rumania. Cambridge, Mass., and London, M.I.T. Press, 1967. 327p. $15.00.

> An extensive chronological survey of Rumania's economy with the emphasis on Soviet-Rumanian economic relations. The only study of its kind in English.

5. History

523.   FISCHER-GALATI, Stephen A. The New Rumania:
       From People's Democracy to Socialist Republic.
       Cambridge, Mass., and London, M.I.T. Press,
       1967. 126p. $6.00. (Studies in International
       Communism, No. 10)

> A dramatic story of post-war Rumania.
> The author analyzes events that led to the
> Communist takeover in Rumania in a stimu-
> lating and lucidly written account.

524.   FLOYD, David. Rumania: Russia's Dissident Ally.
       New York, Praeger, 1965. 144p. $4.50.

> A discussion of national Communism in
> Rumania and of the roots of the conflict
> between Bucharest and Moscow. The
> author has come up with the most notable
> account of the bloodless Rumanian revolu-
> tion that has yet appeared. Students will
> be fascinated by reading the sequence of
> events.
>
> JMH, Vol. 3
> R: Glenn E. Torrey

525.   SETON-WATSON, Robert W. A History of the
       Rumanians from Roman Times to the Completion
       of Unity. London, 1934; Reprint: Hamden, Conn.,
       The Shoe String Press, 1963. 596p. $10.00.

> Although dated, this standard work of the
> early periods of Rumanian history is still
> very useful. It should be included in a
> basic collection for college libraries.

G.   Yugoslavia (Serbia and Croatia)

1.   General Works

526. BYRNES, Robert F. ed. <u>Yugoslavia.</u> New York,
      Publ. for the Mid-European Studies Center of the
      Free Europe Committee, Inc., by Praeger, 1957.
      488p. $8.50.

> A useful reference tool of post-war Yugosla-
> via encompassing all vital aspects of that
> country. Biographical sketches and a
> bibliography increase the book's value.

> JMH, Vol. 30, No. 4, p. 402.
> R: Jean Nelson

527. ETEROVICH, Francis H. and Christopher Spalatin.
      eds. <u>Croatia</u>: Land, People, Culture. Vol. I.
      With a Foreword by Ivan Mestrović. Toronto,
      University of Toronto Press for the Editorial
      Board, 1964. 408p. $7.50.

> This volume offers Croatian geographic and
> demographic statistics, archeology, political
> history, economic development, ethnical
> heritage, folklore, etc. It represents the
> Croatian nationalist point of view which
> rejects the Yugoslav concept, the monarchy
> as well as the Communist state, and em-
> braces the vision of an independent greater
> Croatia.

> JMH, Vol. 37, No. 3, pp. 359-60.
> R: Gunther E. Rothenberg

528. HOFFMAN, George W. and Fred W. Neal. <u>Yugosla-
      via and the New Communism.</u> New York, Twentieth
      Century Fund, 1962. 546p. $8.00.

> A compendium of the main aspects of the
> Yugoslav development under Tito's regime.
> The topics comprise the land of the South
> Slavs, Yugoslav Communism - Soviet style,
> the emergence of Titoism, Titoism as a
> system, the impact of Titoism, problems
> of Titoism. An indispensable reference on
> the development of post-war Yugoslavia.

SEEJ, Vol. 7, No. 2, pp. 228-29
R: Nicholas Spulber

2. Communism

529.   AVAKUMOVIC, Ivan. History of the Communist
Party of Yugoslavia. Aberdeen, Aberdeen University Press, 1964. 207p. (Vol. I)

> This study is instructive not only for the
> history of the CPY but also for that of Com-
> munist parties elsewhere. The author has
> come up with a most useful, readable and
> enlightening work. The study is copiously
> documented and replete with unusually
> valuable social statistics.

> AHR, Vol. 71, No. 1, pp. 254-55.
> R: Ivo J. Lederer

530.   DJILAS, Milovan. Anatomy of a Moral: The Political Essays of Milovan Djilas. Edited by Abraham
Rothberg. New York, Praeger, 1959. 181p. $1.45,
paper.

> This is the translation of the author's 18
> articles from Borba (1953-54) dealing with
> the Yugoslav establishment and Tito's Com-
> munism. An intellectual first, the one-time
> devoted Communist became disillusioned
> with Communist practices. His experiences
> can be multiplied by many similar cases
> attaching particular significance to his
> "confession." Students are urged to study
> and analyze the book.

531.   McVICKER, Charles P. Titoism: Pattern for International Communism. New York, St. Martin's
Press, 1957. 332p. $6.00.

> This book is the best available synthesis of
> the development of Titoism as pictured on

major political and social reforms which
were attempted since 1950. Titoism as a
separate political philosophy claims to be
a halfway house to freedom, a middle stage
between Stalinist Tyranny and democratic
socialism.

JMH, Vol. 30, No. 2, pp. 168-69.
R: Joseph S. Roucek

3. Economy and Economic Conditions

532. PEJOVICH, Svetozar. The Market-planned Economy
of Yugoslavia. Minneapolis, University of Minnesota
Press, 1966. 160p. $5.75.

The author describes and analyzes the system
both in regards to the overall economy and
to individual enterprises. He discusses the
economic theories of socialism and applies
these to the Yugoslav experiment. The book
is written in clear style, well documented
and contributes to the understanding of
post-war Yugoslavia.

CSS, Vol. 1, pp. 144-45.
R: Gunther E. Rothenberg

4. Foreign Relations

533. LEDERER, Ivo J. Yugoslavia at the Paris Peace
Conference: A Study in Frontiermaking. New Haven,
Yale University Press, 1963. 351p. $8.50.

This is the first systematic study of the
Yugoslav question at the Paris Peace Conference in a Western language. This work
largely completes the story of peacemaking
in the mid-Danube area after World War I.

AHR, Vol. 69, No. 3, pp. 768-69.
R: Victor S. Mamatey

534. MacKENZIE, David. The Serbs and Russian Pan-Slavism 1875-1878. Ithaca, N. Y., Cornell University Press, 1967. 365p. $10.00.

> A detailed work of the Serbian-Russian relations in the last quarter of the nineteenth century. Russian Pan-Slavism exploited Serbian national sentiments in promoting Russia's interests in the Balkans. Many aspects of this confrontation are the subjects of this documentary study.

5. History

535. SLISSOLD, Stephen. ed. A Short History of Yugoslavia: From Early Times to 1966. New York, Cambridge University Press, 1966. 280p. $5.95.

> The region-by-region approach resulted in good encyclopedic articles on each region. Useful political summaries and generally good maps characterize this valuable handbook.

> AHR, Vol. 72, No. 3, pp. 1031-32.
> R: Traian Stoianovich

536. HEPPELL, Muriel and Frank B. Singleton. Yugoslavia. New York, Praeger, 1961. 236p. $7.50.

> A brief compendium, published in the series, "Nations of the Modern World, " provides a picture of Yugoslavia that is not thickly covered by national or ideological bias.
> The first part of the book treats the history of the Yugoslav lands up to the outbreak of World War I; the second part covers the history of Yugoslavia since 1918. The popular style of the book suits the purpose and serves well the beginner.

SR, Vol. 21, No. 2, pp. 361-62.
R: Wayne S. Vucinich

537. HOPTNER, Jacob B. Yugoslavia in Crisis: 1934-
1941. New York-London, Columbia University
Press, 1962. 328p. $6.50.

> The essence of the book is the author's
> stylistically impeccable description of the
> total political failure and military unpre-
> paredness of the Western powers, of brutal
> conduct of the Axis partners, and of the
> desperately difficult international and do-
> mestic situation of Yugoslavia. A first-rate
> though unilateral chronicle of events during
> the years 1934-1941.

> SR, Vol. 24, No. 2, pp. 332-33.

538. PALMER, Alan W. Yugoslavia. New York, Oxford
University Press, 1964. 127p. $1.25, paper.

> A brief survey appraising Yugoslavia's past
> and present. The booklet can be recommend-
> ed for high school use and for general intro-
> duction.

539. VUCINICH, Wayne S. Serbia Between East and West:
The Events of 1903-1908. Stanford, Cal., Stanford
University Press, 1954. 305p. $4.75.

> This study treats the Russian and Austrian
> policies regarding Serbia. It is primarily
> an account of how Serbia freed itself from
> dependence on Austria. There is much
> interesting information in this book.

> SR, Vol. 13, No. 4, pp. 613-14.
> R: William V. Wallace

CHAPTER V

JEWS IN EASTERN EUROPE AND RUSSIA

1. Bibliographies

540.   BRAHAM, Randolph L. The Hungarian Jewish
Catastrophe: A Selected and Annotated Bibliography.
New York, Yivo Institute for Jewish Research, 1962.
86p. $5.00. (Joint Documentary Project, Bibliogra-
phical Series, No. 4)

>   AHR, 69, No. 3, p. 769-71.
>   R: Robert Koehl

541.   BRAHAM, Randolph L. Jews in the Communist
World: A Bibliography, 1945-1960. New York,
Twayne Publishers, 1961. 64p. $3.00.

>   A comprehensive bibliography of English
>   literature on the Jewish problem, arranged
>   by countries.

542.   BRAHAM, Randolph L. and Mordecai M. Hauer.
Jews in the Communist World: A Bibliography,
1945-1962. New York, Pro Arte Publishing, 1963.
125p. $6.00.

>   SR, Vol. 23, No. 4, pp. 791-92.
>   R: Solomon M. Schwarz

2. History

543.   BARON, Salo W. The Russian Jew Under Tsar and
Soviets. Edited by Michael T. Florinsky. New York,

Macmillan, 1964. 427p. $7.50.

> This concise survey gives us a well-organized narrative account of Russian-Jewish history from its beginnings in antiquity through the Khrushchev erea. Though lacking a critical approach, the study offers a general background of the Jewish problem in Russia.
>
> JMH, Vol. 37, No. 2, pp. 230-31.
> R: Howard M. Sachar

544. GOLDBERG, Ben Z. The Jewish Problem in the Soviet Union: Analysis and Solution. New York, Crown Publishers, 1961. 374p. $4.95.

> Equipped with personal knowledge, the author discusses all aspects of Jewish life in the Soviet Union and offers some ways of solving certain problems.

545. GREENBERG, Louis. The Jews in Russia: The Struggle for Emancipation. Vol. I: 1772-1880; Vol. II: 1881-1917. Edited by Mark Wischnitzer. Foreword by Alfred Levin. Reissue: 2 vols. in 1. New Haven, Yale Historical Publications, 1966. 213p. $10.00.

> An account of the legislative means which were directed against the Jews in Russia and their reaction to it.

546. MEYER, Peter and others. The Jews in the Soviet Satellites. Syracuse, N.Y., Syracuse University Press, 1953. 637p. $6.50.

> An unbiased study of the Jewish question in East European countries. Topics include the status of the Jews before the emergence of Communist regimes, the development of Communist policy toward Jewish minorities, present status and position of Jews in Eastern Europe.

547.   SCHWARZ, Solomon M.   The Jews in the Soviet
       Union. Syracuse, N. Y. , Syracuse University
       Press, 1951. 380p. $5. 00.

                A pioneering study of the Soviet policy to-
                ward the Jews and Russian anti-Semitism.
                Emphasis is placed on the changing attitude
                of the Soviet regime.

CHAPTER VI

AUSTRIA-HUNGARY (Before 1918)

---

548. CRANKSHAW, Edward. The Fall of the House of
Habsburg. New York, Viking Press, 1963. 459p.
$7.50.

A study of the Habsburg monarchy during its
decline. The events of the last seventy years
are pictured from the viewpoint of Vienna.
It is a stimulating and original survey providing a clearer understanding of the causes
which led to the ultimate disintegration of
this multi-national empire. The lucid narrative will prove to be very informative
and thought-provoking.

549. JASCI, Oscar. Dissolution of the Habsburg Monarchy. Chicago, University of Chicago Press,
1961. 482p. $2.45.

An outstanding treatment of the breakup of
the Austro-Hungarian empire. This study
analyzes and elaborates the causes of its
downfall, stressing the historical forces
involved. The history of Austro-Hungary
has truly found its historian in Mr. Jasci.

550. KANN, Robert A. The Habsburg Empire: A Study
in Integration and Disintegration. New York,
Praeger, 1957. 227p. $5.00.

The author has succeeded brilliantly in his
aim to analyze briefly the character of the
Habsburg monarchy and to clarify the conditions, processes and causes of its gradual
integration and eventual disintegration.
This study may be used as a textbook.

JMH, Vol. 30, No. 3, pp. 276-77.
R: William A. Jenks

551. KANN, Robert A. The Multinational Empire:
Nationalism and National Reform in the Habsburg
Monarchy, 1848-1918. New York, Columbia
University Press, 1950-51. 2 vols. $20.00.

> This work is a most wlecome addition to
> the history of the Danubian area. The
> complex conditions of the Habsburg Mon-
> archy with its various nationalities, enter-
> taining hostility towards one another, are
> the core of the study. The final hour struck
> for all the nationalities of Austria-Hungary
> in 1918 and precipitated the collapse of a
> unique empire.

> SR, Vol. 11, No. 1, pp. 77-79.
> R: Albert Parry

552. KOHN, Hans. The Habsburg Empire, 1804-1918.
Princeton, N.J., Van Nostrand, 1961. 192p.
$1.45, paper.

> The author illustrates how, in an age of
> nationalism, the complex and multi-national
> empire faced the problem of establishing an
> order which would give to various national-
> ities freedom of development and a feeling
> of equality. The general reader and the
> beginning student will especially profit
> from this clear narrative.

553. REMAK, Joachim. Sarajevo: The Story of a Political Murder. New York, Criterion, 1959. 301p.
$5.00.

> A soundly documented account of the fateful
> assassination of the Austrian Crown Prince,
> Francis Ferdinand, in Sarajevo in the sum-
> mer of 1914.

554. TAYLOR, A.J.P. Habsburg Monarchy, 1809-1918:

A History of the Austrian Empire and Austria-
Hungary. London, Hamish Hamilton, 1961. 279p.
New York, Harper & Row, 1965. $1.95, paper.

> A critical and analytical history of the
> Hapsburg empire from its inception to the
> disintegration in 1918. Recommended as
> a textbook for undergraduate courses in
> East-Central European history.

555. WANDRUSZKA, Adam. The House of Habsburg:
Six Hundred Years of a European Dynasty. Trans-
lated from the German by Cathleen and Hans Epstein.
Garden City, N.Y., Doubleday, 1964. 212p. $4.50;
Anchor Books, 1965. 178p. $0.95, paper.

> This scholarly survey offers an introduction
> to Central European history in the form of
> sketchy portraits of outstanding Habsburg
> dynasty. The history of the Danubian mon-
> archy is virtually the history of the various
> East Central European peoples.
>
> SR, Vol. 24, No. 1, p. 133.
> R: Arthur J. May

556. ZEMAN, Z.A.B. The Break-up of the Habsburg
Empire 1914-1918: A Study in National and Social
Revolution. New York, Oxford University Press,
1961. 247p. $5.60.

> Elaborate study of the final years of the
> Habsburg Monarchy offering an informative
> survey of the changing positions of Czech,
> South Slav, Polish and Ukrainian leaders.
> The re-emerging nationalism of the subject
> nations contributed greatly to the disintegra-
> tion of the dual Monarchy. Well-chosen
> photographs bring glimpses of life to the
> reader. A worthwhile historical account of
> the downfall of the Habsburgs and of the
> history of East Central Europe.
>
> SR, Vol. 21, No. 3, pp. 548-49.
> R: Donald E. Emerson

CHAPTER VII

COMMUNISM

———————

1. Bibliographies

557.   HAMMOND, Thomas T. comp. and ed. <u>Soviet</u>
<u>Foreign Relations and World Communism:</u> A
Selected, Annotated Bibliography of 7,000 Books
in 30 Languages. Princeton, N.J., Princeton
University Press, 1965. 1240p. $25.00.

558.   HUNT, Robert N.C. ed. <u>Books on Communism:</u>
A Bibliography. New York, Oxford University
Press, 1960. 333p. $2.70.

       JMH, Vol. 33, No. 3, p. 305-6.
       R: Elliot R. Goodman

559.   KOLARZ, Walter. ed. and comp. <u>Books on Com-</u>
<u>munism:</u> A Bibliography. 2nd ed. London, Amper-
sand Ltd., 1963. 568p. $4.80.

       This second edition lists about 2,500 titles,
       divided into 52 "subject and country sections,"
       of which the first five deal with Communism
       and the world Communist movement, the
       next 20 with the Soviet Union, the next 25
       with Communism and related questions in
       other countries.

       SR, Vol. 24, No. 2, pp. 363-64.
       R: Witold S. Sworakowski

560.   PUNDEFF, Marin V. <u>Recent Publications on Com-</u>
<u>munism:</u> A Bibliography of Non-Periodical Litera-
ture, 1957-1962. Research Institute on Communist

Strategy and Propaganda. Los Angeles, University
of Southern California Press, 1962. 66p. $2.00.

> A list of 947 books and pamphlets in English
> dealing with various aspects of Communism
> for a period of five years.

561.   World Communism: A Selected Annotated Bibliog-
raphy. An Addendum to Senate Document No. 69,
prepared by the Legislative Reference Service,
Library of Congress. Bibliographic Materials
Through September 1963. Washington, D. C.,
Govt. Printing Office, 1963.

2. General and History

562.   BRAUNTHAL, Julius.   History of the International.
Vol. I: 1864-1914. Vol. II: 1914-1943. New York,
Praeger, 1967. 2 Vols. $11.00 and $17.50, respec-
tively.

> In this comprehensive history of the Interna-
> tional the author traces the origins of the
> International in the humanitarian and demo-
> cratic ideals of the French Revolution. In
> Vol. I, he describes the characteristics of
> the predecessor organizations, the ideologi-
> cal and political principles and problems of
> the First (1864-76) and Second (1889-1914)
> Internationals. In Vol. II, Braunthal dis-
> cusses the collapse of socialist ideals at
> the outbreak of World War I; the establish-
> ment of the Third International (The Com-
> intern) and the Labor and Socialist Interna-
> tional, and Trotsky's Fourth International.

563.   COLEGROVE, Kenneth W.   Democracy Versus
Communism: A Teacher's Guide. 2nd ed. Edited
by Hall Bartlett. Princeton, N. J., Van Nostrand,
1961. 442p. $5.75, cloth; $0.80, paper.

This comprehensive and informative book
is designed for high school use. The author
served as political adviser to General Mac-
Arthur in 1954-55.

564. DANIELS, Robert V. ed. A Documentary History
of Communism. New York, Random House, 1960.
2 Vols. in one. $8.75, cloth; Vintage Books,
$3.30, paper.

A critical review of Communist philosophy
from Lenin to Mao Tse-Tung. The greater
portion of this work focuses on internal
Soviet developments. This book is suitable
for quick reference and quotations.

565. DANIELS, Robert V. The Nature of Communism.
New York, Random House, 1962. 398p. $6.00.

By a somewhat different approach the
author appraises the nature of Communism
as a system of industrialization promoted
by a power-hungry party. This well-rounded
presentation may be used in class discussions
on the nature of Communism, particularly
Russian Communism.

SR, Vol. 21, No. 4, pp. 759-60.
R: Robert E. Gamer

566. DANIELS, Robert V. Understanding Communism.
Syracuse, N.Y., Singer Co., 1964. 201p. $2.28,
cloth; $1.32, paper.

This study attempts to answer many complex
questions which Communism is presenting
in historical and philosophical aspects.
Recommended literature for political science
and history courses.

567. DEGRAS, Jane. ed. The Communist International,
1919-1943: Documents. Vol. I: 1919-22. Vol. II:
1923-28. Vol. III: 1929-43. London-New York,
Oxford University Press, for the Royal Institute.

of International Affairs, 1956-65. 3 Vols. $14.40 each.

> A highly comprehensive and reliable collection of documents on the Communist International and Communist parties throughout the world. A basic title for college libraries.

568. DJILAS, Milovan. The New Class: An Analysis of the Communist System. New York, Praeger, 1957. 214p. $4.95, cloth; $1.75, paper.

> The author, sentenced and re-sentenced to anguish in a Yugoslav prison, has given the world an illuminating and devastative treatise on the nature of Communist power. As a former believer in Marx and Lenin, Djilas reveals in his new credo against Communism a penetration and insight possible only to one who is an apostate. This book is highly recommended to all young people.

> SR, Vol. 17, No. 2, pp. 237-39.
> R: William B. Ballis

569. DRACHKOVITCH, Milorad M. ed. Marxism in the Modern World. Stanford, Cal., Stanford University Press, 1965. 293p. $2.95, paper.

> Several specialists, among them Richard Lowenthal and Bertram D. Wolfe, have offered analyses of the various political forms which Marxism has taken on in the twentieth century: Leninism, Stalinism, Krushchevism, Maoism, Titoism and Castroism. This publication is recommended for students of political science.

570. DRACHKOVITCH, Milorad M. and Branko Lazitch. eds. The Cominterns: Historical Highlights; Essays, Recollections, Documents. New York, Praeger, Publ. for the Hoover Institution on War, Revolution and Peace, 1966. 430p. $10.00.

This volume, a result of the efforts of well-
known scholars, sheds considerable new
light on certain aspects and problems of the
Third (Communist) International, the Comintern. The book concludes with a special
documentary section containing material on
the internal problems of some of the Communist parties. This exceptional publication has particular value for students of
political science.

571.   EBENSTEIN, William. Today's Isms: Communism-
Fascism-Capitalism-Socialism. 5th ed. Englewood
Cliffs, N. J., Prentice-Hall, 1967. 262p.

A lucid style, simplified explanations and
comparative treatment of the four ideologies
render this study very useful to the college
student, promoting interest in contemporary
issues.

572.   GRUBER, Helmut. International Communism in the
Era of Lenin: A Documentary History. Ithaca, N. Y.
Cornell University Press, 1967. 512p. $7.50.

A collection of the significant doctrinal statements, manifestos, analyses, tactical decisions, and polemics of the early years of
the Communist movement when world revolution was expected by many. The author provides a concise, stimulating narrative which
ties together and explains the documents and
interpretations included. He traces the developments, conflicts, and splits of the national
Communist parties against the background of
the growing and centralizing Communist
International.

573.   HUNT, Robert N. C. The Theory and Practice of
Communism: An Introduction. 5th ed. New York,
Macmillan, 1957. 286p. $5.50.

A splendid introduction to the theory of
Communism, explaining the doctrines of

Marx, Engels, Lenin and Stalin. The
clarity of the text and the simplicity of
organizations render the study useful to
even high school students.

574. IONESCU, Ghita. The Politics of the European
Communist States. New York, Praeger, 1967.
305p. $6.75, cloth; $2.25, paper.

The author discusses the forms of Communism
in different parts of the world: The Soviet
Union, China, Eastern Europe, Asia, Cuba.
A second part of the study examine the internal
forces in the European Communist states
that check the totalitarian regimes.

575. LAPEDZ, Leopold. ed. Revisionism: Essays in the
History of Marxist Ideas. New York, Praeger, 1961.
518p. $7.95.

Basically a survey of Marxist ideas and the
various revisions of the original doctrine.
The essays treat revisionism from different
aspects of historical perspective. This book
supplies a great deal of information and is
recommended for advanced students.

576. McNEAL, Robert H. ed. International Relations
Among Communists. Englewood Cliffs, N.J.,
Prentice-Hall, 1967. 181p. $4.95, cloth; $2.45,
paper.

A selection of documents representing both
agreements and disagreements on numerous
issues which are challenging Communist
solidarity in international relations. Each
document is accompanied by a brief narrative explaining the nature and the importance
of it. A valuable contribution to the discipline
of international relations.

CSS, Vol. 1, No. 2, pp. 324-25.
R: Peter A. Toma

577. MEHLINGER, Howard D. ed. Communism in Theory and Practice: A Book of Readings for High School Students. San Francisco, Chandler Publishing Co., 1964. 274p. $4.00, cloth; $2.75, paper.

> The author has designed a book geared to the use of secondary schools. Among its special merits are its adaptability to various approaches, topics and units of time in the high school curriculum, its general dispassionate tone and good balance, and its aids for the student.

> SR, Vol. 24, No. 1, pp. 161-62.
> R: John M. Thompson

578. MEYER, Alfred G. Communism. New York, Random House, 1960. 217p. $1.95. 2nd revised edition: New York, Praeger, 1962.

> A scholarly approach to the course of Marxism and Communism since the 1840's. A challenging method of presentation makes this study unique in the long list of titles on Communism published in the last decade.

> AHR, Vol. 66, No. 4, p. 1082.
> R: George Barr Carson, Jr.

579. MEYER, Alfred G. Marxism Since the Communist Manifesto. Washington, D.C., A.H.A. Service Center for Teachers of History, 1961. 22p. $0.50.

> A brief summary of the development of the Marxist philosophy followed by a selected bibliography on Marxism. Useful for quick orientation and reference.

580. MILLER, Richard I. Teaching About Communism. New York, McGraw-Hill, 1966. 355p. $6.50.

> This volume is intended as a handbook for teachers, school administrators and other educators who are responsible for introducing courses on Communism in elementary

and secondary schools. Its scope is broad including a rationale for instruction, a survey of relevant curriculum practices, discussion of the major ideas which should be included in instruction about Communism. Reprints of laws and course syllabi are appended.

SR, Vol. 26, No. 3, pp. 523-24.
R: Howard Mehlinger

581. SETON-WATSON, Hugh. From Lenin to Khrushchev: A History of World Communism. 2nd ed. New York, Praeger, 1960. 447p. $6.75, cloth; $2.95, paper.

This book was originally published in 1953 under the title From Lenin to Malenkov. The author has revised his study and extended into the Khrushchev period. In addition, two more chapters deal exhaustively with the development of international Communism during the late 1950's. An expertly written analytical history of Communism as a world-wide movement. The author dissects the pattern of Communist behavior and the application of Communist strategy and tactics under diverse social, economic and intellectual conditions. An outstanding study on Communism for the students of international affairs.

SR, Vol. 13, No. 2, pp. 285-86.
R: Edward J. Rozek

582. SWEARINGEN, Rodger. The World of Communism: Answers to the 100 Questions Most Often Asked by American High School Students. Boston, Houghton Mifflin, 1962. 278p. $2.32.

This volume represents the first attempt by a scholar to produce a textbook for secondary school use. It is a notable beginning providing a thorough treatment of the subject. The chapters are well organized, dealing in logical progression with ideology, the world movement, the Soviet Union, China, their role in world affairs and the United States. High school teachers have been given an excellent tool for an extremely complex subject.

SR, Vol. 21, No. 4, pp. 761-62.
R: John M. Thompson

583. WOLFE, Bertram D. <u>Marxism</u>: One Hundred Years in the Life of a Doctrine. New York, Dial Press, 1965. 404p. $6.95, cloth; $2.95, paper.

This ably written work deals with some selected aspects of that part of Marx's heritage which reflects his determination to change the world by shaping the development of social and political events. A critical evaluation of Marxism by a former Marxist who saw for himself all the unhappy applications of this utopian and dangerous doctrine. This study, as well as the author's other works, belongs in every basic collection for public and college libraries.

SR, Vol. 24, No. 4, pp. 730-32.
R: Z. A. Jordan

LIST OF JOURNALS AND TRANSLATIONS

For Russian and East European Area Studies

I. Journals (In addition to general periodicals whose
review sections broadly cover a variety
of diciplines related to our interest, the
following titles are recommended for in-
clusion into a library collection)

1. CANADIAN SLAVIC STUDIES: A Quarterly Journal
Devoted to Russia and East Europe. 1967-. Publ.
quarterly by Loyola College, Montreal. Editor-in-
Chief: Charles Schlacks, Jr. Subscription: $6.00
per year. Order from: Prof. Charles Schlacks, Jr.,
Dept. of History, Loyola College, Montreal 28,
Quebec.

2. CANADIAN SLAVONIC PAPERS. 1958-. Quarterly,
1968-. by the Canadian Association of Slavists. Subscription: $5.00 per year. Order from: Prof. Philip
E. Uren, Dept. of Geography, Carleton University,
Ottawa 1, Ontario.

3. EAST EUROPE. 1951-. A Monthly Review of East
European Affairs. Publ. by Free Europe, Inc. Edi-
tor: Francis Pierce. Subscription: $5.00 per year.
Order from: B. De Boer, 188 High Street, Nutley,
N.Y. (The periodical covers the following countries:
Albania, Bulgaria, Czechoslovakia, East Germany,
Hungary, Poland, Rumania, Yugoslavia.)

4. THE EAST EUROPEAN QUARTERLY. 1967-. Pub-
lished under the sponsorship of the University of
Colorado. Managing Editor: Stephen Fischer-Galati.
Subscription: $6.00 per year. Order from: East
European Quarterly, 1200 University Avenue, Boulder,
Colorado, 80302.

5. JAHRBÜCHER FÜR GESCHICHTE OSTEUROPAS.
1953-. (Neue Folge). Publ. quarterly. Editor:
Georg Stadtmüller (Munich). Subscription: DM 58.00
per year. Order from: Verlag Otto Harrasowitz,
Wiesbaden, Taunusstr. 5, Germany. (Articles and
an extensive book review section in German and English.)

6. JOURNAL OF CROATIAN STUDIES: Annual Review
of the Croatian Academy of America, Inc. 1960-.
Subscription: $5.00 per vol. Order from: Croatian
Academy of America, Inc., P. O. Box 1767, Grand
Central Station, New York, N. Y. 10017.

7. THE POLISH REVIEW. 1956-. Publ. quarterly by
the Polish Institute of Art and Sciences in America.
Subscription: $5.00 per year. Order from: Polish
Institute of Arts and Sciences in America, 145 East
53rd Street, New York 22, N. Y.

8. PROBLEMS OF COMMUNISM. 1952-. Publ. bimonth-
ly by the U. S. Information Agency. Editor: Abraham
Brumberg. Subscription: $2.50 per year. Order
from: Superintendent of Documents, U. S. Govt.
Printing Office, Washington 25, D. C.

9. RUSSIAN REVIEW: An American Quarterly Devoted
to Russia Past and Present. 1941-. Editor: Dimitri
von Mohrenschildt. Subscription: $7.00 per year.
Order from: The Russian Review, Inc., Box 146,
Hanover, N. H. 03755.

10. SLAVIC REVIEW. 1940-. (formerly AMERICAN
SLAVIC AND EAST EUROPEAN REVIEW, 1940-1961).
Publ. quarterly by the American Association for
the Advancement of Slavic Studies, Inc. Chairman
of the Editorial Board: Henry L. Roberts. Subscription: $12.00 per year. Order from: Prof.
Ralph T. Fisher, 1207 West Oregon Street, University of Illinois, Urbana, Illinois 61801.

11. THE SLAVONIC AND EAST EUROPEAN REVIEW.
    1922-. Organ of the School of Slavonic and East
    European Studies in the University of London, publ.
    twice a year. Subscription: $8.40 per year. Order
    from: The Secretary-Registrar, School of Slavonic
    and East European Studies, University of London,
    Malet Street, London W. C. 1, England.

12. SOVIET STUDIES: A Quarterly Review of the Social
    and Economic Institutions of the U. S. S. R. 1949-.
    The University of Glasgow, England. Subscription:
    52/6 net. Order from: Basil Blackwell, Broad
    Street, Oxford, England.

13. STUDIES ON THE SOVIET UNION. 1962-. Publ. by
    the Institute for the Study of the USSR in Munich,
    Germany, quarterly. Subscription: $12.00 (air
    mail), $6.00 (regular mail) per year. Order from:
    Institute for the Study of the USSR, Mannhardtstr.
    6, Munich 22, Germany, or: 30 E. 42nd St., New
    York, N. Y. 10017.

14. SURVEY: A Journal of Soviet and East European
    Studies. 1956-. (formerly SOVIET SURVEY).
    Editor: Walter Z. Laqueur. Quarterly. Subscrip-
    tion: $4.00. Order from: Ilford House, 113 Oxford
    Street, London, W. 1. England.

15. THE UKRAINIAN QUARTERLY: A Journal of East
    European and Asian Affairs. 1944-. Publ. by the
    Ukrainian Congress Committee of America, Inc.
    Subscription: $5.00 per year. Order from: The
    Ukrainian Quarterly, 302 West 13th Street, New
    York, N. Y. 10014

II. Translations from original Soviet and East European
    periodicals and newspapers.

1. CURRENT DIGEST OF THE SOVIET PRESS. 1949-.
   Publ. weekly by the Joint Committee on Slavic Studies.

A Selection of the contents of over 60 major Soviet newspapers and magazines, translated into English in full or condensed. Subscription: $50.00 per year. Order from: Current Digest of the Soviet Press, 351 Riverside Drive, New York, N. Y. 10025.

2. DIGEST OF THE SOVIET UKRAINIAN PRESS. 1957-. Publ. monthly by Prolog Research and Publishing Press. Subscription: $15.00 per year. Order from: Prolog Research and Publishing Association, Inc., 875 West End Avenue, New York, N. Y. 10025.

3. EASTERN EUROPEAN ECONOMICS. 1962-. Publ. quarterly by the IASP. Subscription: $40.00 per year. Order from: International Arts and Sciences Press, 108 Grand Street, White Plains, N. Y. 10601.

4. EASTERN EUROPEAN STUDIES IN HISTORY, 1968-. Quarterly, offering selected translations of articles from historical journals in Albania, Poland, Yugoslavia, Czechoslovakia, Hungary, Bulgaria and East Germany. Subscription: $40.00 per year. Order from: International Arts and Sciences Press, 108 Grand St., White Plains, N. Y. 10601.

5. EASTERN EUROPEAN STUDIES IN LAW AND GOVERNMENT. 1968-. Quarterly, offering translations from scholarly sources in the area of law and government from seven countries. Subscription: $40.00 per year. Order from: International Arts and Sciences Press, 108 Grand Street, White Plains, N. Y. 10601.

6. PROBLEMS OF ECONOMICS: Translations from Soviet Economic Journals. 1958-. Publ. monthly by IASP. Subscription: $60.00 per year. Order from: International Arts and Sciences Press, 108 Grand Street, White Plains, N. Y. 10601.

7. SOVIET LAW AND GOVERNMENT. 1962-. Publ. quarterly by IASP. Subscription: $40.00 per year. Order from: International Arts and Sciences Press,

108 Grand Street, White Plains, N. Y. 10601.

8. THE SOVIET REVIEW. 1959-. Publ. quarterly by IASP, offering a cross-section of significant articles from Soviet periodicals in the social sciences. Subscription: $6.00 per year. Order from: International Arts and Sciences Press, 108 Grand Street, White Plains, N. Y. 10601.

9. SOVIET STUDIES IN HISTORY. 1962-. Quarterly, offering selected translations of articles from nine Soviet historical journals. Subscription: $35.00. Order from: International Arts and Sciences Press, 108 Grand Street, White Plains, N. Y. 10601.

AUTHOR INDEX

Includes names of authors, compilers, editors, and translators. Numbers refer to entries, not pages.

SHORT TITLE INDEX

Numbers refer to entries, not pages.

240